No Dogs in Heaven?

Scenes from the Life of
a Country Veterinarian

Robert T. Sharp, DVM

CARROLL & GRAF PUBLISHERS

NEW YORK

No Dogs in Heaven?

Scenes from the Life of a Country Veterinarian

AVALON
publishing group incorporated

Carroll & Graf Publishers
An Imprint of Avalon Publishing Group Inc.
245 West 17th Street
11th Floor
New York, NY 10011

First Carroll & Graf edition 2005

The names of some people and places in this book have been changed. Dialogue from as far back as twenty years ago has been written as accurately as possible. Some details are slightly fictitious, but these stories are mostly true.

Library of Congress Cataloging-in-Publication Data is available.

ISBN: 0-7867-1524-3

Designed by Maria Elias
Printed in the United States of America
Distributed by Publishers Group West

For those whose best friends eat from bowls on the floor,
For those who have never seen an ugly cat,
For those who would rather clean a stall than go to a party,
For those who prefer the company of animals.

Contents

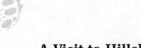

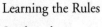

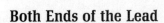

Once in a Lifetime

Continuing Education

Tale End

Index

Acknowledgments

No book crosses the goal line without the help of a good team. I would like to thank them here and now.

Susie Sharp, my wife:
for proofreading all of the stories,
for remembering details of past events,
for her constant assistance in practice.

Carol Cartaino, White Oak Editions:
for her encouragement and enthusiasm,
for smoothing the lumps in the rough syntax,
for offering creative suggestions in all phases of writing,
for being a concerned cat lover, faithful client, and friend.

Reid Sharp and Amy Sharp Schneider, our kids:
for proofreading and computer expertise.

Clayton Collier-Cartaino:
for creative input and opinions.

The Citizens of Highland County, Ohio:
for welcoming a family of newcomers,
for providing a home in the most beautiful part of America,
for allowing me to make a living doing what I love.

The mother in the floor-length skirt with her hair pulled rigidly back from her face said, "Don't be ridiculous. There are no dogs in heaven."

—Southern Ohio woman, expressing indignation at the idea that there might be a place in the hereafter for our canine friends

A Visit to Hillsboro

prologue

The dashboard of the truck was like a scrapbook. There were matchbooks from political campaigns, faded from the sun. Syringes from past injections and dust from a hundred different farms covered the top of the blue metal dashboard. Pens from banks and realtors, pencils from two stockyards, a few coins, paper clips, drug invoices, and an empty bottle of blackleg vaccine were strewn across the base of the windshield.

A veterinarian's truck is no limousine, and Dr. Bill Lukhart's was a little rougher than most. It had been in a head-on collision, and the front end looked like it was sucking a lemon. The fiberglass vet unit on the back was covered with the nicks and bruises that could only come from a million farm calls. This was a work truck that was nearing retirement, and so was the man at the wheel.

Dr. Lukhart had been in practice in Hillsboro and the surrounding counties for over forty years. It was time to take a rest from night calls, cold barns, kicking horses, diarrhea, gunshot wounds, and all the hassles that go with them. It had been a wonderful and interesting career, but he was approaching seventy years old. He hoped reinforcements were near, in fact, sitting next to him.

* * *

Susie and I had been married for ten years and our daughter, Amy, would soon be starting school. Because of graduate school, fulfilling my ROTC commitment by flying in the Air Force, and The Ohio State University College of Veterinary Medicine, we had had to move eleven times. It was time to settle down. Time to find a good place to raise kids. Time to find a real home.

I was in practice in Chillicothe, Ohio, with the best small-animal veterinarian I have ever known. His technical expertise with animals and his skill with people made him a great teacher and good friend, but I was feeling the need to leave the nest. I was an employee; what I wanted to be was the owner of a practice.

At a meeting of the Southern Ohio Veterinary Medical Association (a small group of country vets who meet four times a year to tell stories and eat dinner, with continuing education presentations to follow), Bill had announced that his practice was for sale. I had gone to Hillsboro to talk to him about buying it.

When I got to Bill's office he asked me if I would like to go with him on a short farm call. We could eat on the way. We sat at the Dairy Queen, a block away from the office, and waited for John McKenna, the owner and chef, to finish the preparation of our wieners. He signaled with a wave that they were ready.

"I eat here a lot in the summer," Bill said. "They have great milkshakes, and incomparable wieners." He smiled.

We paid John for lunch, listened to a quick joke (always mandatory), and got back in the truck to eat.

"You don't mind if we drive and eat, do you? We have a

busy afternoon and I'd like to get back early to give you the grand tour." Bill put his butterscotch milkshake on the dashboard so he could steer with his wiener-holding hand and shift the old three-quarter-ton beast with the other one. As we pulled up the steep incline of the parking lot to get on to US 50, the worn clutch slipped, spilling Bill's milkshake all over the dash. He depressed the clutch and rolled us backward so we wouldn't stick out on the road. Then, using a bank deposit slip, he scooped the milkshake on the dash back into his cup and took a drink. Dust and all. He went on talking as if nothing had happened. I liked him already.

"This is the only county in Ohio with two working stockyards," Bill said. "I've worked at this one for over twenty years," pointing as he drove. "The uptown area is still intact and has a lot of historic buildings. Kids drive around these two blocks, cruising, on Friday and Saturday nights. Some are third- and fourth-generation cruisers. 'Mother' Thompson's house is up that street. She started the big temperance crusade that eventually resulted in Prohibition right here in Hillsboro. Ours is the oldest courthouse in Ohio that is still used as a courthouse.

"Over there, in front of Farmers and Traders Bank, is where a funny thing happened. This truck has a loudspeaker on top so that when my wife Martha calls me on the radio, I can hear it even if I'm far away in a barn. That switch by your knee turns it off. I told her before I left home that I was going to Jasper Williams's place, and when Martha thought that I was out on the road, she said over the radio 'Be sure to get your money from Jasper. He's owed us for over three months and I hear he's getting divorced.' Actually I was in the bank. The speaker was on, and it broadcasted that all over uptown. When I came out, people were laughing up and down the street. I had to leave in a hurry. Watch that switch!"

He waved at the driver of practically every car and truck we passed. "You know, I think I could stand on the corner there by the bank and tell you who every stranger in town was. People here know one another. They are all fine people except for a sprinkling of sons-of-bitches, which you'd have anywhere. If you move here, I think you'll like it. Do you guys go to church?"

"We're Presbyterian," I said.

"Me too. A few years ago, the minister, Dean, brought his cat over to be neutered, and as he was pulling out of the driveway of the office, the cat jumped out of my arms and ran down the back hall. When he crashed against the screen door, it popped open. He took off. Dean got home and the cat was waiting for him on the back porch. He called me to say it was the fastest service he'd ever had. I had to explain that I was not quite done yet."

"That white barn over there is where I treated a cow with milk fever that had been down for a week. I don't like to see 'em down even for a day, so I asked the people why they waited so long to call me. It seems they were praying over the cow but she hadn't been healed. I pointed out that in order to be healed by faith, the cow had to be a believer too and she probably was not. The owners agreed and promised to call sooner next time. The cow got all right" (one of Bill's best-known benedictions).

He finished his milkshake and pointed to a red barn we were passing. "I had a little trouble in that barn once. I had to test a bull there for tuberculosis. It was a requirement prior to selling him. The farmer said he was skittish and that I should back the cattle chute up to the barn very quietly. I tried, but I tapped the barn ever so slightly with the chute. There was a loud beller followed by a crash. Then a second crash, and a third. We rushed in to see what had happened. The first crash was the bull blasting through his stall and into another room of the barn. The second crash was the floor giving way under his weight. He was a big Holstein and weighed close to a ton. The third crash was the bull dropping through the floor and landing on the combine that was parked in the basement level of the barn. We looked through the hole in the floor and saw the bull kicking up his heels as he went through the doorway in a dead run for Buford. He didn't turn up for a week. It didn't do the combine much good either. Of course the farmer said it was my fault. He'd told me that I should be quiet. The bull was skittish."

Bill told a new story as we passed each farm. I was like a kid having an adventure book read to him. Bill was a raconteur. I was a willing listener.

"This mailbox belongs to Henry Cashman, and he's terrified of snakes. One day Charlie, my helper, and I were treating cattle here when a blacksnake came out of a hay bale. I thought Henry was going to have a stroke. He screamed like a girl. So for months after that, whenever Charlie or I found a snake in the road, we'd catch it and put it in a feed sack. As we passed his mailbox, we'd take the snake out of the sack and put it inside. Henry told us all summer about how a family of those damn snakes had made a nest in his mailbox. He'd go out to get his mail, and a new snake would fly out at him. He had theories concerning why a snake would want to climb up and get in his mailbox. Charlie and I ruined it when we found a box turtle on the road and put him in the mailbox. Henry finally smelled a rat, and gave us hell for a year after that."

Up and down the beautiful hills he drove the old truck. They had been there together for a lot of miles. He warned me of bad curves, and as we descended Prospect Hill, he told of the day his cattle chute came off the trailer hitch, and went past him going downhill at 70 mph. "It flipped over about six times and ended up on that front porch."

Bill loved Hillsboro and told me that, of course, I would be a Rotary Club member. He described an annual telethon that raised money for crippled children. Every cent stayed in Highland County. No administrative costs. "They don't do that in the big cities."

"Of course if you want to go to the city, we're pretty close. Hillsboro's in the middle of everything. You can have a heart attack, and be in the best heart care center in America after a fifteen-minute helicopter ride."

"Oh, hey, this is the farm where I had a cow fall down a well. You should have been there for that . . ."

I don't remember now what we did on that farm call, or even whose farm we visited. I had been thinking about the possibilities of practicing here. I had been a city mouse and now I wanted to try something else. As I drove back to Chillicothe to report to Susie about my interview with Dr. Lukhart, I was wondering if we would be accepted in a small town like Hillsboro. I was wondering if a steel-town-reared, small-animal veterinarian could actually do large-animal farmwork in the country. I wondered if I could run the business end of a practice well enough to pay the bills. It was a big step, and in retrospect, an exciting time.

I didn't know then that Bill would become my large animal mentor, my fishing partner, my gardening instructor, and my friend. And Hillsboro would become home.

Training
the Rookie

The one-ton Holstein bull stood in front of me like a black-and-white locomotive. "Willie's in a lot of pain, Doc. He hasn't put that foot down in two days and he won't even let me touch it. What are we gonna do?" Strange, that a man who had been around cattle all his life would be asking me for help!

I *should* have said, "How the hell should I know? I'm a steel-town kid raised on bowling alley 'pastafazool' and I've never touched a living bull before today." But I was the *expert* here, so what I said was, "You hold onto that ring in his nose and I'll put a little anesthetic into his tail vein. When he's asleep we'll get a good look at that hoof."

As I walked around Willie's outhouse-sized hindquarters and lifted his tail I thought, I'm about to stick a needle into an animal that could pulverize a pickup truck. If he kicks me I could have the shortest career in veterinary history.

To a fledgling veterinarian, every farm call is an

adventure. Easy problems, hard problems, they're all the same—a challenge, a chance to try out some of the things learned in ten years of college. While small-animal practice (dogs and cats) was more familiar to me (and took up the majority of my day), the large-animal calls were more fun. Dealing with huge animals out in open pastures on beautiful farms was better than anything I had ever envisioned as a student. I looked forward to each day with the enthusiasm of a rookie just called up from the minor leagues.

This first group of stories is about how an optimistic young veterinarian was taught by kind people and patient animals.

As for Willie—he took the shot "like a man" and I was able to find an abscess in his hoof wall caused by a puncture of some sort. He and his owner were happy. And so was I.

Living Proof

I'd never met a man who wore only cutoffs and wing tips until I met Mr. Harris. But then I hadn't been on many hog calls yet either. He came to the door of his trailer with a cigarette hanging from his mouth. "They're out back" was all he said as he went down the wooden steps of his six-foot-square porch and lit out down the path to the back field. By the looks of his tan he wore cutoffs and nothing else most of the time. Wing tips were optional.

I had been called to come and treat some feeder hogs that "were so sick they could hardly stand." While I'd been driving to Harris's, I'd been thinking about all the hog diseases I'd studied that might cause a mass collapse of ten

Hampshire hogs. I'd had no real experience with pigs; I'd had a city-kid upbringing, and little interest in swine medicine in vet school. My intention as a student had always been to be a small-animal vet, so the classes that dealt with stuff like this were academic exercises for me, taken only to meet graduation requirements. But after a year of experience in a small-animal practice, I had purchased a practice from a retiring vet that involved about 40 percent farmwork. Here I was, City Kid following Wing Tips down the garden path to a destiny I had never foreseen. Hog work. I was about to test my education against the real world. Books vs. pigs.

The path led past a garden and into a grove of maple trees. It was obvious that Harris didn't want the hogs near the house. They weren't anywhere in sight. We walked another half mile across a bean field and back into another small wooded area. There they were! It looked like a scene from a professional mud-wrestling match. A fenced area had been constructed in a rough square using three strands of barbed wire wrapped around trees. Two hundred twenty-five square feet of mud. No grass, no weeds, no rocks, just mud. In one corner was an empty feed trough. In the center of the arena were ten black-and-mud-colored hogs piled up like they had just tried a "quarterback sneak."

"They've been like that for a week. They only get up to come over to eat. And then they're so sick they can't walk a straight line."

"Have any died?"

"No, and none seem to get better, either."

I started to climb over the barbed wire to examine one of the patients when I looked at the mud again. Too deep for my boots; they were only a foot high. I'd seen those movies where the quicksand sucks you under: "Do you think you can take the temperature of one of these hogs?" It was Harris's mud. He could get in it.

"No problem," he said as he slid under the middle wire and sank his wing tips into the ooze. A surprised hog let out a "hummph" as the thermometer was inserted. While it was "cooking," Harris's wing tips gradually disappeared. Down and down they went. "It reads 101.8 degrees." Normal.

He assured me, as he made his way back to the fence, that they had been vaccinated, and fed daily. Over in the corner of the woods was a fifty-five-gallon drum and bread wrappers scattered everywhere. "What's in the can?" I asked.

"That's their slop. I stop at the bakery on my way home from work every night and get all the day-old bread they throw away. Them pigs love it! I just put it in the drum and add water. When it's feeding time I scoop it out into the trough."

I walked over to the drum and lifted the lid. The smell was familiar but definitely not bread. Bread fumes don't burn your eyes. A lightbulb went on in my head. The bread and water at the bottom of the drum was never scooped out. It stayed in the bottom and fermented. I don't know what "proof" this stuff was, but it was strong medicine. Strong enough to make ten 150-pound hogs drunk.

This hog medicine isn't too tough, I thought, as I was packing my stuff into the truck. The owner smiled as I told him that the hogs would be OK once they were "on the wagon." I was glad I'd been able to make a diagnosis, and that I hadn't disappeared into the mud. This had not been a case of books vs. pigs after all, just common sense vs. no sense.

Driving home, the Highland County sky was turning bright red. It was a warm July evening and I was feeling pretty good. Probably better than the hogs would be feeling the next day.

Compensation

Rain was coming down for the third day in a row. The first two days didn't matter, but this was my day off and I had great plans. Not anymore. The windshield wipers on the old Ford three-quarter-ton truck were slapping off the rain as well as they could, but visibility was minimal. The road to Ft. Hill was wonderful for motorcycling. No straight stretches, no flat spots, just an endless series of curving hills winding through the southeast corner of Highland County. On a sunny day this was motorcycle heaven. In an old vet truck without power steering, a hole in the floor-boards in the perfect spot to keep your left leg wet, and headlights that pointed wherever they liked, it was more like having a twenty-mile wrestling match with the road.

Ft. Hill is a prehistoric Indian earthwork that comes complete with a state park where people like to picnic and hike on nice days. But today there were no cars in the parking lot, and today—my day off—I had been called to treat a calf with "scours," that is, diarrhea, which in calves can be life-threatening if untreated. This calf was only a few weeks old, and was more at risk than a calf that weighed 800 pounds.

According to the owner's directions, their trailer was directly across from the entrance to Ft. Hill. And so it was, an old singlewide trailer parked at an angle, with its tail end hovering over a stream that ran through the property. I had heard about this sewage-disposal technique from the old-timers, but I thought that in this time of regulation and environmental protection the "self-flushing toilet" was a thing of the past. The toilet in the trailer simply dropped its contents into the stream. When you don't have running water in the house, there are other cleanliness issues. This was not a good sign.

Bales of straw were placed around the bottom of the trailer for insulation against the wind. A pair of plastic flamingoes, white with age, strutted their stuff on rusty legs. Old lawn furniture and car parts were everywhere. The place looked like it had been abandoned, or should have been. A concrete frog held the front door open as the rain came down. It must have been hot in there, even though it was just above freezing outside. The path from my parking spot to the front door was a mixture of puddles and mud. Mud from the adjoining pasture had been tracked up the wooden steps and into the trailer. I was almost afraid to meet these people.

"He's in here, Doc," said the huge woman who appeared in the doorway. Mrs. Brill, I presumed. I went up the steps, thinking Mr. Brill was inside, and as I entered I was met with shimmering heat and a concentrated odor of diarrhea. There, on the couch, lay a 150-pound Angus calf. Perched on the back of the couch was a rat terrier, rhythmically barking at me, the intruder. He defended his castle, bouncing and barking, drooling and snarling, like a miniature version of the guard dog at Hell's Gate.

"Shut up, Spot! Git yer ass off there," Mrs. Brill shouted, smacking him off the filthy blanket on the back of the couch. He hit the floor and now came around after me. Great.

He skidded in the mud on the floor and was intercepted

by his mistress's foot, kicking him under a chair that was next to the fifty-five-gallon drum they used as a "wood stove." Spot now had a new post to defend.

"This calf of Ralph's ain't been right since we bought him at the stockyard last Monday. Nothing but scours, and we got that good milk replacer at the feed mill." The couch gave a good demo of the type of diarrhea he had. Very smelly stuff. The courageous Spot continued his defensive tune.

"We need to give the little guy some fluids," I told Mrs. Brill as I took some equipment out of my bag.

"Ralph's in town at court today. They caught him driving again and he might go to jail this time."

She had dropped the bait and I couldn't resist. "Why would he go to jail for driving?"

"He had his license taken away for DUI. This was the second time he's been caught driving since then."

"How did he get to town today?"

"He drove."

I got the bag of fluids running as the calf, Spot, and I listened to what sounded like an episode of a soap opera.

"It's a great time for it too, since I'm on disability from the pants factory. My elbow got hurt running the big press." She bent her elbow to show me and the ash from her cigarette fell on the calf.

Good therapy, bending that elbow, moving the cigarette to her mouth, I thought. She'll be better in no time.

"You know I can't put too much into this calf," she said, walking to the kitchen. "We paid a hundred for him and I don't think he'll live anyway."

The kitchen was a work of art. In a trailer, the kitchen is an area, not a room. This area was a still life of pots, pans, utensils, and dishes, both clean and dirty, stacked up into what looked like a room divider starting at the floor. I suspected that the items on the bottom might be the clean ones, thanks to Spot's tongue. "Can you use some hot water, Doc?" Mrs. Brill said, pulling a pan from the middle of the wall-o-pans. Miraculously, nothing else moved. She was experienced. Water was added from a jug and the pan was put on top of the drum to warm. I guess she thought I needed it for something. She must have seen the movie in which the famous line "Get towels and plenty of hot water!" was first spoken.

The calf began to improve immediately, trying to roll from his side up onto his chest. I gave him an injection of an antibiotic, and had just sat down to get some medicine for diarrhea out of my bag when Mrs. Brill said, "While you're here, Doc, we got a cow in the back with mastitis too. Looks like a tit might be gonna rot off."

When you have other things to do, the dreaded, "while you're here, Doc" is never welcome. At least, this time, the cow would be outside. I looked over to see if Spot was ready to attack or if it was safe to get up. "Where were you planning to put the calf?" I asked, hoping there was a barn or outbuilding somewhere on the "farm."

"Leave him right there. He won't hurt nothing."

We agreed on that point. When I went down the steps, Spot followed at a distance that allowed him to watch. Behind the trailer, tied to a tree, must have been the cow Jack had traded for the bag of magic beans. The old brown Jersey looked fifty years old and had an udder that needed a sling to keep it out of the mud. "Which teat is the bad one?" I asked looking at four disastrous droopers.

"The front right quarter is a-drippin' pus," said Spot's

benefactor. "We had her give to us last year so we could raise calves with her. So far it ain't worked out too well."

The cow's teat dripped pus as I watched. "I have some mastitis medicine in the truck. You'll have to put one of these syringes of antibiotic up in the teat every twelve hours," I said walking back in that direction. Spot followed at a distance.

I gave Mrs. Brill a box of mastitis syringes, some injectible antibiotics, a list of instructions, and a bill. As I got back into the truck the rain slowed to a sprinkle. I backed out of the lane while Spot stood in the middle of the driveway, standing guard.

Four months passed, and I had almost forgotten about Mrs. Brill until Melissa, my technician, reminded me that our monthly statements had been ignored and the Brills's bill remained unpaid. Big surprise. The mail probably went into the homemade wood stove. A reminder was again sent, this time with an idle threat attached. We sometimes threatened to turn someone over to small claims court, but we almost never followed through. The court would give a judgment that we were owed the money, which we knew already, but getting the money was the real problem. Out went the threat in the next day's mail.

Two weeks passed and Melissa interrupted me in the exam room. "Dr. Sharp, there's a lawyer on the phone and he says it's important."

I excused myself and answered the phone, "Dr. Sharp."

"Dr. Sharp, my name is Vincent Fagnano and I represent Mr. and Mrs. Ralph Brill."

I thought for a moment and then remembered the Brills. "Yes sir?"

"I do not want you to take them to court for payment of their medical bill since Mrs. Brill's Worker's Compensation claim has been approved, and your bill will soon be paid in the distribution." His tone made it sound like he represented royalty.

This made no sense. Why would Worker's Compensation pay a veterinary bill? Then I knew. They would pay if they thought I was one of Mrs. Brill's physicians. She had listed me on her insurance claim as a family doctor.

"Mr. Fagnano, are you aware that I am a veterinarian and my bill was for a calf with diarrhea?"

Silence . . . then we both began to laugh. "What a tribe," was all he said.

The Hill

I had been in practice in Hillsboro less than a week, and was struggling to get everything organized into a manageable group of problems. The office interior needed paint. Construction had begun to convert a large-animal surgery area that had been used for storage of many years of accumulated stuff (too good to throw away, yet not good enough to use) into exam rooms and office space. The building had been designed and built in the 1950s, and wasn't suited to small-animal practice.

Anyway, the truck was the country vet's office. If you didn't have it in the truck, you didn't need it. As time passed and different large-animal problems arose, you added tools, drugs, and equipment that you needed, but didn't have on the last call. After forty years, you had it all. And so I inherited a rolling toolbox that looked like a veterinary Home Depot. There were large pieces of equipment in the back that gave me no clue as to their use. But I knew that I probably would need them someday.

I was going out on a call after supper one evening, heading down the Belfast Pike, when I noticed that traffic was stopped up ahead. A Highway Patrol car was by the side of the road, and cars were being waved into line for safety inspections. Not good.

"Bill's Bomb" would never pass. I was, of course, waved into the line and moved up to take my turn.

Things went well at first. I had a driver's license, the horn worked, the lights apparently came on.

The Ohio state trooper next asked me to put on my bright lights.

"Excuse me," I said as I opened the driver's door of the old Ford. "I have to do that down there," I said pointing to the left front wheel well. I walked to the front tire and grabbed the foot switch that was dangling behind it by a fraying wire. Having fallen through the rusted floorboards, it was easy to find. I pushed on it, and presto, bright lights.

The trooper shook his head. "Doc, you can't do that. There's no way this truck's going to pass a safety inspection. The headlights don't even point at the road. One of 'em is aimed at the other. The grille is attached with bailing wire. How many miles does this thing have on it?"

"Dr. Lukhart claims that it's turned over twice. I guess it would have about 230,000 miles on it now."

"That explains a lot. I thought it looked familiar but I didn't recognize you. So this was Bill's old vet truck. Did he tell you about the time he came out to my place and. . . . "

Everyone knew Dr. Lukhart. He had practiced his

entire career in Highland County, and his father had practiced here before him. He knew every farm, every back road, every fishing pond, and the history behind them all. He was one of the reasons I had wanted to practice here.

I was born and reared in an Ohio steel town and worked my way through college as a welder. Beautiful southern Ohio was unknown to me until I attended Miami University in Oxford. When I was considering the purchase of Bill's practice he told me, "Rob, most people work in the city all their lives, and when they finally get to retire, they move out here in the country. I already live here and work here and I have all my life. What could be better?" He was right.

"Doc, if you promise not to take this bomb out at night, I'll let you go without a safety violation ticket, but you won't get a window safety sticker either," said the man in uniform.

I promised. Who in their right mind would drive this truck after dark? A new truck with a veterinary bed insert was on order.

"Do you have the same phone number as Doc Lukhart if I need you?"

"Sure do, and thanks a lot, Sergeant Green." I left the roadside stop.

I was on my way to Gordon Mathews's farm to help an Angus cow deliver a calf. Gordon lived quite a distance from Hillsboro, down the roller coaster Belfast Pike, across Flat Run Road and up May Hill. He was a retired fire captain from the city who bought a farm and moved to serenity. His farm was in the rocky hills where plowing wasn't possible, and most farmers raised sheep or cattle among the cedars. It had snowed earlier in the week and the roads were a little slippery, especially near May Hill. The hillsides were white and beautiful.

"Hi Rob!" said Gordon as I pulled alongside his barn. "This might be a little tricky since she's in the high pasture. We'll have to take all the stuff we'll need up the hill. I don't think your truck will make it."

Gordon's home was lovely and literally built around a two-story log house from pioneer days. The entryway was the former living room of the log house. It could easily be featured in a magazine of unique homes.

The sheep pastures were behind and next to the house and barn. The cattle were kept across the road in a pasture that was on the top of a very steep hill that ascended from the valley floor. The path to it through the woods was twisty and very steep, climbing and turning through the trees like a slalom course. A four-wheel-drive vehicle was mandatory equipment.

"How long has she been in labor?" I asked.

"Most of the afternoon. The calf feels really big, and she had trouble last year. We have our choice of vehicles to get up there, Rob. We could take my truck but the hill is slippery and muddy too. We could take the snowmobile, but the equipment will be hard to carry, especially the calf puller. Or we can take the bulldozer, and have a lot of room for equipment. It's up to you."

"If you think your truck can make it, that would be my choice. It's getting dark and windy and the heater might feel good."

"Good point. We might need the headlights coming back down. The dozer's lights don't work."

We unloaded a calf-puller, obstetrical chains, a stainless steel bucket and disinfectant, two lariats, a bottle of lubricant, some uterine boluses for infection, five syringes, a bottle of tranquilizer, a bottle of antibiotic, a few spare needles, and my drug bag, just in case. We then loaded it all in the back of Gordon's four-wheel-drive pickup. Obviously, the snowmobile would have been cramped. We drove across the road and started up the hill.

The path was only a little wider than the truck and started to the left through a grove of cedars. It was getting very dark now and snow was falling. Windshield wipers became necessary. A sudden turn to the right and the ascent began. "This gets steeper on up the hill. We need to get up a head of steam or we might start to slide at the top," said Gordon.

Get up a head of steam? He was driving like A. J. Foyt in a pickup truck. Dodging trees, weaving back and forth, up and up we went, bouncing and banging. Near the top we were in a forty-five-degree climb when the tires started to slip.

"I don't think we're gonna make it this time, Rob. Better hold on to something. We're going back down."

"What?" was the best I could answer. Going back down? In the dark? Backward? How could he see? The lights were in the front.

"Grab something, Rob—we're sliding backward." Gordon faced the rear, and with his left hand on the wheel, looking over his right shoulder, he steered the sliding truck as it lost all traction and started speeding up, going the wrong way. If we hit a tree, it wouldn't be pleasant. I slid down in the seat and grabbed the dashboard. Back and forth he steered. It seemed like slow motion and a bad dream.

Gordon pumped the brakes to control the slide and did a masterful job of not killing us both. I guess four-wheel-drive trucks can't climb everything.

As we approached the bottom of the hill, Gordon

looked over at me and said, "Christ, Rob, you're as white as a sheet!"

It took me a minute to get up enough spit to respond. "Let's take the bulldozer."

We drove back to the barn and unloaded the truck. All the stuff was packed on the big Caterpillar and Gordon fired up the diesel motor. Smoke belched from the stacks as the big yellow beast came to life. "This will make it to the top," I said, almost as a question.

"No sweat," replied Gordon. "Hold on to something."

When Gordon says hold on, he means it. I'd never ridden on a bulldozer before. They ride like you'd expect. Very loud, growling, clanking, squeaking, smoking, unstoppable power. There was no stopping us this time.

"Hey, Rob, can you see the path?"

I didn't want to hear that. "Are you kidding?" I asked in disbelief.

"Actually yes. This dozer and I made the path. I don't need lights."

We crawled to the top without headlights or trouble. We found the cow without using headlights but not without trouble. A black cow in the dark. We had counted on the truck headlights to find her. Oops.

There were thirty black cows in the forty-acre pasture, but this one had a white star on her forehead. Only about ten had that. When we found her, the calf by her side was still wet and wobbly. Snow was falling on us all. Welcome to May Hill, kiddo.

"I guess she got sick of waiting for us." I said, not feeling at all bad that this night was about over.

"I'm sorry, Rob. I could have sworn that she couldn't deliver it on her own."

We descended the hill on steel tracks and never slipped an inch. I loaded the equipment back in the truck while Gordon went in to make coffee. The fireplace felt wonderful and sitting next to it, we repeated the night's adventures to Caroyl, Gordon's wife. We all laughed as Gordon tried to re-create the look on my face when we started to slide.

After being invited to bring Susie back for a house tour, I said good night and walked out to my truck. Then I remembered Sergeant Green and my promise. I walked back to the house and knocked on the door.

"Forget something, Rob?"

"Gordon, can I borrow your truck?"

Alone

Down in the hills, past the church at Marble Furnace, there was a farm owned by an old woman. She had raised Hereford cattle for as long as anyone could remember, and because of her crusty nature, did it pretty much alone. Help was hard to find, and the help that she did find never suited her. She was a step beyond independent.

I had heard stories about Louise Lewellen from the locals, but I had never met her. I was not her regular veterinarian, and after hearing some of these tales, I was just as glad. I answered the phone at seven AM on my day off.

"Dr. Sharp, this is Mrs. Lewellen, down in Adams County. I can't reach Dr. Davis, and I have a heifer trying to have a calf. She was bred by accident and is really small. Will you please come down and help me?"

"Of course," I said clenching my teeth. Louise Lewellen on my day off. Perfect. Where was that piker Davis hiding? "Can you give me directions, Mrs. Lewellen? I get lost easily in Adams County."

"Can you find the Tranquility Wildlife Area?" she asked. "It's only four or five turns from there."

Her directions were exceptionally clear, and I left the house thinking that I would have no problem, even though this was a twenty-five-mile drive. It was spring, and the dogwoods and redbuds were blooming, adding pink and white splashes to the bright green new leaves of the hillsides. It was a perfect day for a drive, warm and fragrant with the country morning dew.

I passed an occasional vehicle parked in the grass along the roadside; mushroom hunters were in the woods looking for morels. I rarely had time to hunt for mushrooms, but I had clients who gave them to me when the harvest was good. Beer battered and fried, nothing's better.

I made the turn off Marble Furnace Road and followed the township road exactly 3.4 miles, as Mrs. Lewellen had instructed. I turned on to the gravel lane, and followed it about a mile through some rugged outcroppings of rock. It emerged into a beautiful green valley.

Her farm was only suited to cattle farming, since the steep, rocky ground would never allow plowing or planting. The valleys between the hills were lush with new grass. My first impression of the scene in front of me was that it should be on a calendar.

I pulled the truck up next to the barn and saw Mrs. Lewellen for the first time. In the middle of a twenty-acre meadow was a bent-over silver-haired form in jeans, a red flannel shirt, and high rubber boots, leaning on a walker. She lifted the walker and took a step, lifted the walker and took a step, inching toward the far end of the pasture. I opened the gate and drove the truck out into the field. Driving up behind her, and thinking she wouldn't hear me coming, I was afraid I might startle her, so I pulled alongside her at a safe distance. "Mrs. Lewellen?"

"I thought you'd never get here, so I was going out to help her myself."

It was not yet eight AM and I had made excellent time. "Can I give you a ride?" I asked the wrinkled cattlewoman.

"She's right over there against the fence."

I looked over and saw a 700-pound Hereford calf. Surely this was not the heifer that was trying to give birth. She was a baby herself.

"Dr. Sharp, this is what happens when you can't get good help. The stinkers that I hired to fix my fence took the money and did practically nothing. The bull walked right through an old broken part. I guess they thought that I wouldn't see their work, since I'm almost ninety and don't see well. The bull saw it. Now this heifer is in trouble. You go ahead. It would take me longer to climb into the truck than to walk. I'll meet you at the heifer."

I parked the truck near the fence, got out, threw a rope over the heifer's head, and tied her to the fence post. Opening the vet unit on the back of my truck, I put on a shoulder-length palpation sleeve, lubed it with a lot of slickum, and inserted my hand into the birth canal. I could feel the calf and the problem. Some calves are in a bad position for delivery and need to be rearranged. Some are just too large. This one was too large.

I had already decided on a course of treatment when Mrs. Lewellen arrived with her walker. On the front of the walker she had a white woven basket with pink flowers on it. It was probably originally on a girl's bike. In it were several strands of bailing twine and a kitchen knife. "What were you going to do with the twine?" I asked, already knowing the answer.

"If you hadn't arrived in another ten minutes, I was going to pull the calf myself."

"Well, it's not quite that simple. I can only feel the calf's nose jammed against the brim of the pelvis. Its head will never fit through, not to mention the rest of the calf. This is the equivalent of a thirteen-year-old, one-hundred-pound girl trying to deliver a sixteen-pound baby."

"So they'll both die?"

"Not if we do a caesarian section."

"Dr. Sharp, I hate to lose her but I won't be of much help to you. Can you do it alone?"

"I hope so. There really is no good alternative. We can't cut up the calf and remove the pieces because the head is too large to pass through the pelvis. I suppose euthanasia is another possibility."

"What?"

"We could shoot her."

"Oh, hell no!"

"Well, let's get the calf out of there. I'll give her the anesthetic and then get everything we need to use on the tailgate of the truck. It can be our Mayo stand (the small table placed near a surgical patient to hold instruments, named for its inventor, Doctor Mayo. Most surgical instruments are named for the surgeon who invented them—Metzenbaum scissors, Backhaus towel clamps, Crile hemostats, and so on).

"This is exciting. I've never seen this done before."

"What's even more exciting, Mrs. Lewellen, is neither have I. I came from a small-animal practice and have done this quite a few times on dogs, but never on a cow. She will be my first."

"You just pretend this is a big dog then, and I'll help you all I can."

I drew up a measured amount of xylazine and gave it in the large vein on the underside of the tail. Within a couple of minutes, the heifer was anesthetized for surgery.

Humans, dogs, cats, and most other species have C-sections done through an incision on the ventral midline, that is, from the belly button on down. Cow C-sections can be done this way also but it's not the preferred method. Making an incision in the middle of the abdomen would require the cow to be on her back, which is pretty stressful considering the hundreds of pounds of stomach contents inside.

In cows, the incision is usually made in the right par-alumbar fossa, which is the indented triangular area of the side right behind the ribs. In this case, the surgery can be done with a local anesthetic while the cow stands there chewing her cud.

I wanted a combination of the two methods. I wanted her asleep and on the ground, but I would make the incision on her right side. Mrs. Lewellen couldn't help me lift the calf up and out of the uterus with the cow standing, and I couldn't do it alone. The calf would weigh over a hundred pounds and lifting it five feet in the air was impossible for a guy with wimpy arms. With the cow on her side, removing the calf would be easier to do by myself.

I clipped the hair from the area over the incision site, and scrubbed it with surgical soap. I poured alcohol on the area to rinse off the soap, and unpacked the sterile instruments that would be used for the surgery. Sterile packs of instruments, needles to close the wounds, heavy absorbable gut to close the uterus, nylon suture for the skin, all laid out in the probable order of need. I turned to Mrs. Lewellen and said, "Are you ready for this?"

"Let's go. You just tell me if you need something and I'll get it."

I put on my gloves, picked up the scalpel, and got ready to blaze new ground. There was an expression at vet school that was used frequently in surgery labs. "See one, do one, teach one." This meant that the instructor would demonstrate a surgery. It was then your turn to do it. After doing one yourself, you could then teach it to another student. I never got to see this one. I just skipped right to "do one."

As I incised the skin of the right paralumbar fossa, I was amazed at the thickness of the layers. This stuff was as tough as cowhide. It was, in fact, cowhide. I cut through the peritoneum and was into the abdomen. It was easy to sort out the treasures within. The cow has four stomachs, and they all look very different. There is also a mile of intestines in there. The uterus was the large muscular object with the calf in it. So far, so good. Mrs. Lewellen leaned on her walker and watched every second. "Would you rather sit down in the truck? I can holler if I need you," I said, thinking she might pass out or get sick. I have had people pass out from watching a one-inch spay incision being made in a cat. This was a big one, maybe two feet long.

"I wouldn't miss this for the world. Don't worry about me."

I tried to pick a spot on the uterus that would be easy to suture after the calf was removed and the uterus contracted. The muscles of the uterus contract quickly and it would be difficult to suture an incision that was drawn into a place I couldn't reach. I also wanted the incision near the front feet of the calf so that I had two handles to grab. I made my choice and I made the cut.

Fluid poured out of the uterus as the membranes surrounding the calf were incised. I grabbed the calf's slippery front legs and guided them toward the incision. Holding the legs in my right hand, I pulled the head through the incision with my left. Now was the big moment. "Here we go."

I lifted straight up on the calf, pulling it through the incision in the skin, and laid it on the ground in front of Mrs. Lewellen. "I'll take it from here," she said. "I've done this part for seventy years." She wiped the fluid and membranes from the calf's face and plucked a long weed from the ground in front of her. She stuck the weed in one of the calf's nostrils and moved it in and out. The calf sneezed and blew liquid from its nose. Breathing was regular and deep. The calf was alive.

"Oh look, Dr. Sharp. It's a girl!"

I nodded. I was trying to close the huge incision before the cow woke up. It would not be good for her to stand up and dump intestines and other abdominal contents out of the large open hole I'd made. I closed the uterus first, using heavy chromic gut that would eventually be absorbed by her body. I then closed the peritoneum and subcutaneous tissues with the same suture material. The skin would be tougher to close since it was thick cowhide. I used a large curved cutting needle like upholsterers use on heavy cloth, and closed the skin with monofilament nylon that was tough enough to tie up a cabin cruiser. I didn't want this incision to come apart.

By the time I was finished, Mrs. Lewellen had the calf rolled up on its chest and looking good. All the membranes composing the afterbirth had been removed. She was a pro.

A few curious cows had come over to the fence to watch. I started to clean up the equipment and put it all in a bucket to take back to the office when my patient stood up. I gave her a huge dose of antibiotic by injection, placed a handful of antibacterial boluses into her uterus, and gave her a dose of oxytocin to cause the uterus to contract even more forcefully, dumping out any remaining liquid. Then I stood there trying to think of what I might be forgetting.

Mrs. Lewellen urged the calf toward her mom and she stood up and started to nurse. This was textbook perfect, and I'd never read the book. Talk about lucky.

"I think they'll be fine," said Mrs. Lewellen. "Let's go back to the house and get a little breakfast. My checkbook is there too."

On the outside, her house appeared to be made of white boards. On the inside, it was a huge two-story log home, built in the early 1800s. We ate coffee cake and drank milk as she told me some of the history of the farm and some of the people who had lived there. On the walls were pictures of a young girl showing cattle and holding rosettes of accomplishment. Pictures of a young man. Her home was filled with antiques and memories.

"You know, Dr. Sharp, in all the years that I've been raising cattle, I've never seen that done."

"You know, the conditions were ideal. She was out in a clean spring pasture, not a manure-filled barn. It wasn't raining or snowing. You caught the problem before it was too late, also. A less vigilant person would have lost them both."

"Nonsense, you saved them and I'm very grateful. This was really fun. You know I'm very old and people around here think I'm nuts already. Usually no one will help me. When my husband died, almost forty years ago, I didn't know what to do with the farm. I loved it here but everyone told me to sell it. They all said that a woman alone can't raise cattle. I even had a marriage offer, but I knew he only wanted the farm. I learned to trust myself and do almost everything by myself. I am fussy, but people around here think I'm unreasonable. My son lives in the city and when I die, before my body is cold, he'll sell this farm that's been my life. What a shame for him. He thinks that a little more money will make him happy. Oh well. Be careful going home and take these with you." She handed me a paper sack filled with mushrooms.

"I'll be back in two weeks to take out the stitches. Call if you have trouble."

When I returned to remove the stitches, the calf and her mom were standing in the pasture next to the house. I was surprised to see how well the calf was growing. I was also surprised to see Dr. Davis's truck at the farm.

Mrs. Lewellen signaled to me from the porch, and I went up to greet her. "They're doing great, but come inside. I have a little job for you."

Dr. Davis was at the kitchen table drinking coffee. "Hey, Rob, we have another heifer trying to have a calf, and I came to watch you in action."

"Don't pay any attention to that blowhard Davis. Both of you listen to me. I want you both to witness my signature on a new will. I know it will be contested, and my son will claim I'm crazy. If you are asked to testify, will you say I'm nuts or not?"

We both agreed that she was not nuts.

"I'm leaving my farm and probably a half-million dollars, give or take, to my son, but only if he lives here and doesn't sell the place for ten years. If he sells the place, the proceeds and my other money will go to the charities that I've listed. This was drawn up by my lawyer, but I wanted the two of you to witness it. I know that you'll do the right thing, and people will believe you when he starts squealing. Who knows, maybe he'll learn to like it here."

We all signed.

I remained Mrs. Lewellen's back-up vet for a few years, but time and diabetes finally caused her to enter an assisted living facility. She lasted less than a month. To the best of my knowledge, the will was never contested.

I haven't been back to Mrs. Lewellen's place since her death. I wonder who lives there now.

Down in the hills, past the church at Marble Furnace, there was once a farm owned by a very nice lady.

Stormy Night

It had rained all day and there was no letup in sight. I had just finished my last appointment when the phone rang. Melissa called out to me:

"I have a man on the phone who says that he can't reach his vet down in Adams County and his buggy horse ran into barbed wire. He says the cut is over three feet long, and right across the horse's chest. He has an accent—I think he's Amish."

I picked up the phone and spoke with the man briefly. He was indeed Amish. A fence had lacerated his horse's chest from shoulder to shoulder, and he was more than twenty miles away, south of Seaman. I told him to get the horse in out of the rain, and that I would be there in about forty-five minutes.

I had been in practice in Hillsboro for less than a week after leaving a small-animal practice in Chillicothe. I knew none of the roads, none of my clients, and I'd had very little practical experience with horses. I had never treated a horse that was not in a university setting. It was pitch black outside, lightning flashing every few seconds, and windy. Very windy.

I had never met an Amish person before either, so this was going to be a new experience in every respect. The Amish were a mystery to me. I had seen them as a kid when we took my older brother to Scout camp near Cleveland. I knew (or thought) that they dressed funny and kept to themselves. They plowed with huge horses. They rode in buggies. They had only one curtain in each window of their houses. To top it all off, they spoke another language. Since I had grown up in a factory town and had no contact with the Amish, all this was enough for me to include them in the frightening category of "things that go bump in the night." They were different, mysterious, to a kid. Nothing had happened yet to change my opinion.

The trip to the farm was no more confusing than any other call to a place I'd never been. Two wrong turns, and a stop at a country store for directions, and I was there. Mr. Miller was waiting at the barn.

What is that thing in his hand? I thought. Did the storm cause a power outage? All of a sudden I realized why he was holding a Coleman lantern. The Amish don't use electricity. The plot thickens.

"Thank you for coming, Doctor," Mr. Miller said with a German accent. "This gelding is my favorite horse. I've had him for fifteen years and he has never run into a fence before. I think he was scared by the booming thunder."

Flashing lightning, booming thunder, pouring rain continued.

"Is he inside here?" I asked, heading into the barn.

"Ya, he is."

"I'd like to see the cut. Can we turn on some lights?" I asked, thinking that maybe they had electricity for emergency use.

"We won't need lights. We have a good lantern."

In a barn, on a stormy night, in the dark, with a wounded horse. If only my Air Force flight crew could see me now.

I followed his light into the barn and up to a large chestnut gelding that was cross-tied in the walkway. Mr. Miller held up his light and he was correct on all counts. It was indeed a good light source and provided me with a clear look at the largest, deepest cut that I had ever seen (or have ever seen since). If I extended my fingers straight ahead and inserted my hand into the wound, the cut edges would have extended almost to my elbow. The laceration went across the horse's chest like a grille goes across the front of a car. Four feet across. The muscle was hanging down making the wound gape open at least a foot. There was a strong familiar odor in the air.

"What's that smell? Is there a fuel spill in the barn?"

"That's coal oil that I put into the wound to keep the flies away."

Not only would that damage the exposed tissue, but it was flammable. And we were holding a lantern next to it.

"Let's back up a little before we catch the horse on fire. We don't want him to blow up too. He's had a bad enough day."

Mr. Miller howled with laughter. He thought my comment was really funny. "Don't you worry. I've done it many times and no horse has burned to the ground yet!"

"This may take quite a while to suture. Can we hang the lantern up somewhere or do you want to hold it?"

"You stitch, I'll hold."

Flashing lightning, booming thunder, pouring rain continued.

I mixed a cocktail of drugs to give the horse that would serve as a tranquilizer and painkiller. Three drugs in the same syringe. I gave it intravenously and the big gelding's head lowered. He was very calm and now I could inject some local anesthetic along the wound.

Suturing a huge wound in layers is not so much difficult as time consuming. Several hundred stitches were required and took a couple of hours. During that time, Mr. Miller told stories about his family, his farmwork, and life in general. He held the lantern all the while, giving me a surgery light that moved as I needed it. He was funny, kind, and by the time the last stitch was placed, I had a new understanding of Amish people. They are like the rest of us, with a couple of extra quirks.

I packed up my instruments, left a bottle of antibiotic and some syringes, and gave final instructions. No more coal oil. Mr. Miller was very appreciative and paid me in cash and a berry pie.

I drove home in the same storm I'd driven out in, and when I pulled into the office parking lot to unload the surgery packs and equipment, something seemed different. It was the front porch of the office. The next door neighbor's maple tree had blown down and crushed it. I could deal with that the next day. I needed some sleep.

Mr. Miller removed the sutures himself. I couldn't call him on the phone to check on the horse. No phone. I did learn a year later from a neighbor that the horse had healed with hardly any scar and was back pulling his buggy without problems.

There are now many Amish people in Highland County, too, who sold their farms in Pennsylvania at a good profit and purchased larger ones here, in southern Ohio. We have become the new "Amish Country."

For the last twenty-five years, I've enjoyed my trips to Amish farms. The mystery of the Amish has disappeared.

Learning the Rules

If a cow is going to die, and you touch her, you will get the credit for her death. This is a rule of veterinary medicine taught to me twenty-five years ago by a friend who practiced for over forty years. It had been taught to him by his father, an Ohio State University veterinary graduate of the 1920s. There are many corollaries but all revolve around the same general rule, which is as true today as it was ninety years ago: Human nature is unchanging. The first case I had that reinforced the rule occurred early in my career.

Mrs. Williams called the office on a spring morning in 1982. "Dr. Sharp, my husband asked me to call and see if something can be done about a sick cow that we have here. She's been sick for about two weeks."

This is usually a tip-off to failure. You'd like to say:

What the hell have you been doing all this time? Now she'll croak for sure. Why don't you call the neighbor who's been your "consulting specialist" all week? I don't want any part of this. But you don't.

"I'll be out sometime before noon," I replied, knowing that I had other patients to see before I could go. It was not the cow's fault that she was owned by a negligent human.

When I arrived, the cow was unable to stand, and was propped up on her chest by a hay bale so she wouldn't bloat. She hadn't eaten in two weeks, and she was covered with flies. Her temperature was two degrees below normal and she was twitching. "I really think she's about to die," I told Mrs. Williams.

"You've got to try something, Doc. My husband would hate to lose her. We've already lost her calf."

"Can you tell me what happened to her?" I asked.

"The neighbors helped us pull the calf two weeks ago. It was hard on her. We had to use the tractor. She hasn't been right since. We went to the feed mill and bought some medicine for her. Henry's been hittin' 'er hard with 'conabiotic.' We've been puttin' poultices on them bed sores."

It's hard to look at an animal in this condition and not try to help her. That's why I was asked to come out. So I tried. I gave her intravenous fluids with electrolytes, calcium, phosphorous, a large dose of an anti-inflammatory drug, and a modern antibiotic. I told Mrs. Williams that I thought the cow would die, but to carry water and feed to her anyway.

I was eating supper the next night when the phone rang. "Dr. Sharp, this is Mrs. Williams. I wanted you to know that after you were here, the cow got up and walked to the barn. My husband let her out this morning to the pasture and she staggered and rolled down the hill behind the barn. We just found her there dead. My husband says it must have been the medicine that killed her and he ain't paying the bill."

The abbreviated account of this, recalled forever after at the feed mill, would be, "Yeah, we had a cow that had trouble having a calf once. We had Doc out and she died."

If a cow is going to die, and you touch her, you will get the credit for her death.

This can be broadened into what I call The Rule of Permanent Responsibility: *Once a veterinarian touches an animal, he is forever responsible for everything.* We all know that the reason a dog gets fat has nothing to do with her five-thousand-calorie-a-day diet of ham, eggs, braunsweiger, liverwurst, fried chicken, and potato chips. It's because she was spayed. We also know that the four-month-old puppy was perfectly house-trained until she was vaccinated. Years of house-soiling followed. It had to be the shots.

Another example was recently added to the list. The phone interrupted my dinner: "Doc, my cat's hemorrhaging from where you neutered him!"

A sick feeling came over me. This is the kind of phone call that causes an immediate adrenaline release in any surgeon. The last thing you ever want is for your work to do harm. "I'll meet you at the office as soon as you can be there."

The caller took his time as I sat for half an hour waiting for him. Surely the cat will be dead by now, I was thinking. Then an old Buick pulled up.

Into the office walked Don Johansen with a cat carrier. I asked him to spell his name, got out the cat's records, and aimed him toward an exam room.

He pulled a drenched cat out of the carrier. "We just

put him down in the tub to give him a bath when the water turned red with blood!"

I looked down at his record. I had neutered this cat three years earlier. No possible way was he bleeding from his incision. Further examination revealed the problem.

"Mr. Johansen, the flea poop on your cat dissolved and turned the water red. He's not bleeding."

The Rule of Permanent Responsibility: *Once a veterinarian touches an animal, he is forever responsible for everything.*

And then there is The Rule of Least Compliance. *Just because you say something should be done, doesn't mean it will be done.* Never is the full number of pills given until the last one is gone. Every six hours means before and after work. Written instructions are left in the client's car.

We were about to leave the office for lunch one day when the phone rang: "Melissa, Julius is on his way to the office with the beagle Dr. Sharp spayed yesterday. Her incision came apart and she's dragging her intestines."

This is the worst possible kind of phone call. The dog could die and it might be my fault. Was the suture not tied tightly enough? What could have happened? Could it be fixed?

The wait for Julius was unbearable. He seemed to take forever. When he finally pulled up in his pickup truck, his dog, Molly, was jumping around in the truck bed. Julius was dressed in hunting clothes with mud up to his knees and a whistle around his neck. I went straight to Molly.

Picking her up from the bed, I rushed her into the treatment room. "What happened, Julius?" I asked on the way in.

"She seemed like she was a little slow on the rabbits this morning. We'd only been out for a couple of hours when she didn't want to hunt anymore. I looked at her incision and seen that stuff sticking out."

Another adrenaline release hit me, but for a different reason this time. "Julius, didn't you even look at the written instructions that were sent home with her yesterday? The part about keeping her quiet for two weeks? Didn't your wife tell you what Melissa stood at the front counter and explained? She never should have been hunting. She should have been at home resting."

"She wanted to go this morning. She acted fine."

Her incision was separating just a little and a harmless piece of fat was protruding. It was easily repaired and Molly was fine.

Just because you say it should be done, doesn't mean it will be done.

There is one yet-unnamed rule to go. It relates to events that occur without warning, with blame assigned to the veterinarian, who had no chance at preventing them. This rule is in developmental stages, and an example follows.

"I can't believe that animals can be diabetic just like my uncle Les! I never thought I'd be giving shots to my cat! My hands are shaking so badly I can hardly do this," said Mrs. Dooles.

"It really is pretty easy. You won't have any trouble," I tried to explain. Taking her newly purchased package of insulin, I opened the box, removed the instruction sheets that surrounded the bottle, gave a quick demonstration of mixing the contents without making a "milkshake" of it, and drew up three units into the small syringe. "This needle is so fine that Cletus will never know you're giving him a shot. Go ahead, just put it under the skin."

"You're right! He never flinched! This will be easy!"

"Now remember to come back at five o'clock and we'll check his blood glucose level to see how the insulin worked."

At five o'clock Mrs. Dooles was in the exam room with Cletus.

"How did he feel today?" I asked.

"He's been great, but now I have to go back to the drug-store and get a new bottle of insulin."

"At three units a day the one we used this morning ought to last for months," I said.

"Well, as I was carrying Cletus up the back porch steps, I dropped the bottle and it broke. If you'd left that 'packing material' around the bottle like it was wrapped up at the factory it wouldn't have broken. It's your fault."

Of course.

Stockyard

Had Norman Rockwell painted a rural Southern Ohio portrait, he might well have chosen as his subject a stock-yard arena on sale day. Theater seats in rising concentric half-circles, filled with farmers in bib overalls and flannel shirts, jeans and western plaids, weathered faces under ball caps, all watching the central sawdust-covered sale ring and the animals that come and go. Some are sellers, hoping for a high sale price. Some are buyers hoping to win with a low bid. All sit elbow to elbow, chewing tobacco firmly in place, watching the progress of the sale. Dust, ammonia fumes, and the smells from the stockyard kitchen fill the air.

The auctioneer sits at a raised platform down in front, wearing the obligatory white Stetson, and singing out a language that only the parties around the room can translate. Next to him sits the bid recorder. The animals are sent into the ring on one side of the auctioneer, paraded around, and taken out the other side with the bidding complete. No buyer needs a number since they're all known to the auctioneer and bid recorder. The sale occurs every week, and just like the pews in church, the seats are occupied by the same warm bodies at each meeting of the faithful.

The sale ring is where the action happens, but it's the smallest part of the stockyard building complex. The door that opens to allow animals to enter the ring is the end point of a large maze. Hundreds of pens and pathways made of rough-sawn lumber are formed from posts and gates that interconnect to allow movement of animals from any one area of the yard to any other area simply by swinging gates open and closed. There are central aisleways, but the movement of animals in an efficient order for sale requires the skill of an orchestra conductor. Some are coming to the ring, and some are leaving and going back to other pens at the same time. When ten 800-pound steers leave their pen, they can't be running into another group of steers and getting mixed up with them in an aisleway. Everything is organized so the animals move in groups that are carefully separated from one another.

Highland County is the only county in Ohio with two working stockyards. One is only three blocks from downtown, and the other is on the west edge of town near my office. Their weekly sales are three days apart, so if you want to sell livestock and get some money, or buy a few head to raise, you're never more than a couple of days from a sale.

In addition to the weekly sales, both yards have special sales. Feeder pig sales may bring in four thousand pigs to be sold to buyers who will raise them until they reach slaughter weight. In the fall, feeder calves are sold in the yards to be fattened in feedlots over the winter. On the day of the sale, calves are trucked into the stockyard, weighed, registered at the office, sent into the maze of pens, and then sold that evening at auction. Yard workers glue numbered identification tags on the backs of the calves. It's possible that two thousand head of cattle will be sold at a feeder calf sale between seven PM and midnight.

Some of the buyers want to have their new purchases vaccinated, castrated, treated for parasites, or dehorned, or to have a variety of other operations performed before they take them home. Enter the stockyard veterinarian. Notes are left with the women at the main office who do the tally work and handle the finances, instructing the veterinarian about work to be done before the trucks come to get the cattle in the morning. Working a feeder calf sale is an all-night job for a veterinarian, and since Dr. Lukhart had done it for years, I inherited the job. The regular stockyard veterinarian who worked the weekly sales didn't want the night job, and I needed the work and exposure as the new "doc" in town. So I became the feeder calf sale night man for a while.

The gavel hits the table for the last time, the office workers finish the paperwork, the hired hands go home, the truckers pull out, carrying the cattle that need no treatment, and the coffeepot finally gets turned off. When the last person goes home, the veterinarian is left with a handful of instruction sheets, a stockyard full of cattle, and a very lonely night of work ahead of him.

At midnight, the yard activity drops to zero. A surreal environment is created by the hundreds of lightbulbs hanging from cords, the dust of thousands of cattle in the cold night air, steam coming off the backs and out of the mouths of the calves, the smell of sawdust and urine, and the noise of hundreds of homesick calves moaning for their mothers. Most of the humans are gone.

To be treated, cattle must be moved through the maze to either the "head gate" where they are walked through a narrow pathway to be individually caught by the head in a sliding pipe gate, or to a squeezing pen for vaccination and treatments not requiring so much restraint. The squeezing pen just concentrates the group.

The veterinarian needs a helper, and mine was Nick Busch. Nick and I looked over the work orders for our first night together in the yard. The manager of the stockyard had recommended Nick to me, and said that since he knew the locations of the pens in which the cattle were kept, he would be of great help in finding the "patients" to be treated. Nick could use the work and I could use the help. I had no idea where pen B26 or C254 or any of the more than two hundred pens in the yard were located. He also knew how to move the groups from any pen to the head gate or treatment chute, and back again when we were done. I could not have done the job without Nick.

Nick had risen to the top of his abilities as a helper in the stockyard. He was slow moving, probably due to his 400-pound size, and not a quick thinker about most things. He wore jeans with no belt, held up by once-bright yellow suspenders, and an age-perforated T-shirt with a racing stripe of chewing-tobacco drool down the front. He spoke softly in a language that was mostly mumble through a huge chew, with a Kentucky twang thrown in to confuse me a little more. But he would work all night, do the best he could, and didn't mind helping a rookie veterinarian who had never set foot in a stockyard until that week. Thank God for Nick. We were quite a pair.

"Nick, why don't we start with something easy. There are twenty-two steers in pen B11 that need to be vaccinated and wormed. Let's go find them and move them into the treatment chute. Can you find B11?"

"I fink it's offa heer," he said, moving slowly to the main aisleway.

We opened the first large gate and walked around it, closing it behind us. You actually built pathways as you went down the maze. Sometimes you would swing a gate open and leave it open, in anticipation of sending cattle down that way later. At other times the gate would need to be closed. I followed Nick as we opened twelve large gates, swinging some open, closing some, as we went. B11 was just ahead.

Nick opened the gate of B11, and twenty-two steers weighing about five hundred pounds each and having a circular back tag with 3344 - 3366 on them, were, God help us, turned loose in the yard. This was the correct lot, since backtag numbers were always on the work order. They headed down the aisle and I watched in amazement as the group walked down the path we had made, through the maze, and followed it straight to the treatment chute. Nick had a gift, indeed! I mixed the vaccine, loaded it in a pistol syringe, and as I stuck each calf, marked it with an orange paint stick to let me know which had been done, in case they shuffled themselves in the pen. Nick opened the end gate of the treatment chute and the steers walked out and back up the maze. Nick said something but I didn't know what it was. I followed as the cattle walked through the pathway of gates and back up to B11. We closed the gate behind them and went to the next work order. Mission accomplished.

Seven hundred more cattle to treat, but it was only 1 AM. Nick and I went to C33 for the next batch.

For the next five hours we moved cattle and did whatever treatments were requested. I was learning both how to find cattle (even when they were in the wrong pens, or unmarked pens) and how to interpret some of Nick's speech. We were actually becoming an efficient team.

One of the work orders called for the dehorning of a Holstein bull that had been left over from the weekly sale. It had no location.

"Nick, where do they keep bulls? There isn't any pen number on the sheet."

"Mullbens," he said.

"Where?"

"The mullbens offa heer."

Got it! The bullpens . . . but where are they? "Where is he, Nick?"

I followed him through eight gates, opening, closing, opening, closing until finally, in the middle of the maze, was a group of fortified chutes that were big enough to hold one bull each. The chutes had a door or gate on each end, and they were narrow enough so that the bull inside couldn't turn around. They looked like fortified packing crates for one-ton bulls. Only one of the wooden vaults had an occupant. A huge black-and-white shape filled the center chute. It had to be our patient, since one end had a large ring through the nose, and the other had testicles the size of cantaloupes.

Nick looked a little worried, but I thought he was just showing the natural concern one has for any large animal. I looked toward the head gate where we wanted him, and it was a straight shot down the aisleway. We just needed to release him and move him to the head gate pen and into the head gate, close the metal rails, trapping his head, and remove his horns.

I opened the front door of the bullpen, and the bull blasted out like a one-ton bullet out of a gun barrel. Nick climbed up on a gate with the thundering grace of a 400-pound ballet dancer, getting out of the way as the bull spun around like a rodeo bull and took aim at me. He looked like every illustration of a raging bull—snorting, pawing the ground, shaking his head, and getting ready to smash some-thing. It's an exhilarating feeling to have a bull this size in an aisleway with you, about to crush you like a bug. I had found the center of the maze and just released the mythical Minotaur. A tactical blunder. He didn't want to walk to the pen like the big calves, and he wasn't about to be herded anywhere. He had different ideas.

He charged past me and jumped over a five-foot-high gate, smashing the top board in the process. It occurred to me that if he could clear a gate that high, he could possibly clear any gate in the yard and, God help us again, get loose in TOWN. I hadn't felt like I was in this much trouble since the fourth grade.

While the bull pawed and spun, I ran to the truck and grabbed my black bag. It held a bottle of tranquilizer that might save us all. I loaded two cc's in a pistol syringe and went after the bull, putting the bottle in my pocket in case I needed more.

It's amazing how brave you can be when you're des-perate, and at fault. I opened and closed gate after gate, heading to the last known spot where the bull was loose. I covered the distance between us as fast as I could run. My hands were shaking, and I felt like a hurdler with palsy. I jumped into the aisleway with the bull, ran up to him without even slowing down and stabbed his giant ass with the tranquilizer. He jumped and spun around, as I went over the top of a gate to hide. If he got loose in town, at least he would go to sleep somewhere and not run amok and have to be shot, or worse.

Nick came up and said something that I couldn't understand. I was out of breath, tired from the night's work, and probably in trouble with several people, including the bull's owner. I panted for a while with my hands on my knees, and as I looked up, Ferdinand lay down and went to sleep. The sun was rising outside the stockyard.

I decided that I would dehorn him while he was sedated, so I went to the truck and got all my stuff. And as the one-ton giant snored, I sawed off his horns and pronounced him cured. As he began to wake up, we encouraged his still slow-moving rear end, and moved him, staggering, back into the bull pen and slammed the door. What a relief. But I did make ten dollars for the dehorning job.

We had one more pen of cattle to vaccinate before we could call it a night and the cattle trucks arrived.

"Nick, where is pen U77?"

Again, he said something I didn't understand, and started off across the yard. We opened and closed, open and closed, gate after gate, pen after pen, heading to an area of the yard that we hadn't seen all night. I followed my leader like a beagle puppy behind his favorite little boy. When we finally stopped and I closed the last gate, I realized that we weren't in a cattle pen at all. I had just followed Nick into the men's room.

Bubbler

"Nothing will ever go right at some farms, and this is one of them," Bill said as we pulled into the driveway. "I don't know if it's bad management, or just bad luck, but I know it's true. For almost forty years I've had trouble here. They're such nice guys that you almost wish they'd call another vet. I think you'll inherit the same situation. I don't think it's me."

The Jackson brothers farmed 240 acres with their father. In addition to grain farming, the boys raised hogs and milked about a hundred Holstein dairy cows. They were hard workers, but not prosperous farmers. Dr. Bill Lukhart was with me just for fun. Even though he was retired, he still enjoyed riding along and telling stories. As we passed farm after farm, he would point and tell of some interesting case or disaster that occurred there. When he heard that I was going to the Jackson farm, he thought he should come.

"LeRoy said when he called that this cow wasn't due for a few weeks, but when they went out to the back pasture to check on the dry cows, she was having trouble. What kind of trouble, I don't know."

"Bad trouble, I can tell you," Bill said. We drove up past the milking parlor and started to look for the boys. At the top of the hill we could see someone in bibs waving his arms. "There's Laddy." On we drove until we reached him.

"She's out there in the back pasture. Thanks for coming, Doc. I think she may have gone into labor a day or so ago. Hi Bill! Haven't seen you for a while. I guess today I got a pair-a-docs."

Laddy hopped in the cab with us and pointed to a large

black-and-white bump on the top of the hill. The patient. The old truck bucked and bounced as we went over the rough terrain of grass clods and cow ruts. Every bump caused the chains, calf-puller, buckets, drugs, and junk in the fiberglass vet unit to bang and rattle. We steered around a collection of rusty abandoned farm implements littering the field.

"Can she get up?" I asked.

"She hasn't since we found her. She's been right there all morning."

As we got close, she looked our way but didn't move. We parked close to her head so, if necessary, we could tie it to the truck. Bill was the first to walk around to the cow's business end. He looked up smiling and said, "It's a bubbler."

It's easy to smile when you're retired and get to watch someone else handle a difficult problem. His smile was the smile of relief. Bill was off the hook this time. I walked behind the cow and looked down at the head of a dead calf, swollen to twice its normal size and protruding from the vulva. The scary thing about this was that the rest of the calf was similarly swollen. You just couldn't see it. It was an "emphysematous fetus," filled with gas, and decomposing inside the cow. A "bubbler." No wonder she didn't feel too chipper.

Obviously, it would not be a simple matter to get this calf out of its mom. A caesarian section would cause gallons of septic fluid from the uterus to be dumped into the cow's abdomen. This would surely kill the cow, who was not a good surgical risk anyway. The calf could not pass through the birth canal in the normal way, even with force from a fetal extractor. This left one option: The calf, dead already, would have to be removed in pieces. The dreaded fetotomy, on a bubbler to boot. Bill smiled.

A fetotome is a simple device. It consists of a piece of stainless pipe about two feet long through which is passed a loop of wire that has tiny teeth on it. The loop is put around the body part to be removed. A grasping handle is attached to each free end of the wire at the other end of the pipe. Most work is done by feel, well within the uterus. The handles are pulled alternately until the part is severed and removed. The pipe protects the tissue inside the cow. A simple procedure but easier said than done. I put on shoulder-length plastic gloves and prepared to do battle with the bloated corpse.

"What are you gonna hafta do, Doc, hit her in the head with the pipe?" Laddy asked, laughing.

I was glad they were enjoying this. "I can hardly get my hand past the calf's head. This is really a tight squeeze." I inched my hand along the calf's neck toward the cow's pelvis. It would go no farther. "Obviously the head has to go." The uterus was pressing against my hand like a vise.

We pulled the loop out of the end of the fetotome, extending enough wire to pass around the calf's neck. Laddy took up the slack on the handles as I guided the wire behind its ears. "Go ahead and start," I said reluctantly, holding the pipe.

After four or five alternating pulls on the wire saw, it cut through the skin causing a hissing noise and a putrid smell. The gas under the skin of the calf was escaping. Another thirty pulls and the head dropped on the ground. The cow never moved. She seemed uninterested in the whole process. But her uterus continued its relentless expulsive pressure.

Bill said, "If you give her a spinal, she'll stop trying to push it out. That may give you more room to work in there."

He was right, of course. Forty years of experience teaches you a lot. On the other hand, we had a new drug that worked well and didn't require the accuracy of a spinal injection. One ml given in the tail vein and Myrtle the cow was sound asleep. No more uterine contractions and straining. The body of the calf now could be pushed back into the uterus.

As I lay on my right side with my left arm inserted in the cow to my shoulder, now sorting out parts was a little easier. By the same process of looping the wire saw over different appendages, the major parts of the dead calf were removed. One bloated, smelly, rotting piece at a time. This calf had been dead and stuck for days.

As the last large piece popped out, with traction from all of us, a flood of fluid followed. The procedure had taken over two hours, and my left arm was almost numb. My coveralls were soaked with fluid from the uterus. Myrtle was waking up as Laddy said, "Well, that wasn't as bad as I thought it would be. Do you think she'll be all right?"

"If she doesn't die from infection. We'll put her on a high dose of antibiotics and you'll have to dump her milk for a month or so," I told him. You can't sell milk from a cow that is on antibiotics. It gets into the milk and dairy farmers are very careful not to contaminate an entire holding tank or, worse yet, the milk truck that picks it up. One cow's milk can cause a dairyman to have to buy the whole truckload if contamination is discovered.

"She's getting up!" Laddy said as the cow raised her rear end and wobbled to her feet.

I gave her a few more injections—one drug to cause her

uterus to contract and empty, another for shock—and dropped a handful of antibacterial boluses into her uterus. Just as I was dropping in the boluses, Myrtle started to bolt. We'd never tied her to anything and I guess she'd had enough of being interfered with. She stepped in my bucket, crashed into the right front headlight of the truck, breaking it and bending the fender, and took off across the pasture as if nothing had happened.

Laddy's brother Lonnie drove up to see what was happening. "Why was that cow running across the field? What did you guys do to her?" he laughed. "It's a good thing you're here, Doc. I just drove by the barn and there's a cow down with milk fever. She just staggered into the pond and her nose is just out of the water. She may be a tough one to treat."

I looked over at Bill. He was grinning again.

Horsing Around

The Cleveland Indians were a real powerhouse team for the first time in my life. I had been a loyal fan, even though they had struggled since I was a Cub Scout. Just as I sat down to watch the amazing new team in the first game of the American League playoffs, the phone rang.

"Doc, this is Robbie Sheppard. I've done a real dumb thing."

The introduction of the players began as I thought, calling me now was another dumb thing.

"I tried to geld my neighbor's horse and I think I have some intestines hanging out. Can you come over and save him? I feel real bad about this. The horse belongs to a kid and

I thought I could just do him like a bull calf. Ya know? He wouldn't hold still and the kitchen knife I was using slipped."

It wasn't too surprising that he would attempt this surgery. Most farmers castrate their own calves. A spirit of self-sufficiency is part of the lifestyle. They fix their own tractors, weld their own milking stalls, build their own outbuildings, and if necessary, deliver their own children. Since the first farmers cleared the forests of America and planted crops, they've taken care of their own problems. They invented "do it yourself."

"Is he bleeding very badly?" I asked.

"Not that I can see, but the flashlight batteries are getting weaker and I can't see much of anything."

"Can you keep him from lying down? We don't want him to go down and further contaminate anything hanging out. I can be there in about half an hour. Keep him up if you can."

I was still trying to understand the thinking process that tells you: Go ahead, stand behind a half-ton horse wearing steel shoes and cut his testicles off with a kitchen knife. He won't hurt you. He'll just stand there quietly and let you do it.

And I'll bet the owner of the horse got up that morning and thought: Today's the day I'll have Robbie, the toothless neighbor with the ninth-grade education, attempt surgery on my daughter's favorite animal.

And I'm sure Robbie thought: I'll call Doc. He won't be watching his beloved Indians and will be more than happy to come out in the dark and fix my mess. After all, it's just a horse with unknown body parts hanging out, and a slight attitude problem. He'll enjoy the challenge!

I hung up the phone, put on my coveralls, left the introduction of players, and went to my truck. I made sure I had plenty of anesthetic and antibiotics. My truck had an old fiberglass vet unit on the back that carried water, a small refrigerator, and all my tools, instruments, drugs, chains, and buckets in a variety of compartments. If what Robbie said were true, I might be needing most of my equipment.

Marshall is a small crossroads in the county that still boasts a high-school boys' state championship basketball team in 1928. The town was a little bigger then, and its largest building still standing is a gymnasium. There's a gas station with no gas, a church now abandoned by its Presbyterians, and a few homes. The lane I was searching for was about a mile out of town, marked by a mailbox. Corn was very high now and lined the road like the pathway of a maze. As I turned down the mile-long lane, I could see only corn on each side of the truck and the sky canopy above. It was a little spooky, but a great night for baseball.

Kerosene lanterns were visible in the distance. I drove toward them, onto a grass lawn, and down to the crowd that had gathered. I parked twenty feet from the patient, got out of the truck, grabbed my flashlight, and went to the scene of the crime. "How's he doing?"

"Pretty good, I think. He's been real calm and just standing here waiting for you," Robbie said.

A woman was holding the horse's lead shank. I walked over and rubbed the stallion's nose. He seemed like a pretty understanding guy. I kept my hand on his body as I walked back along his left side. Horses like to know where you are and appreciate a constant reminder so there are no surprises. I didn't want any surprises either. When a 1200-pound animal jumps, he may land on you. As I passed the beam of my flashlight along the underside of the horse, I was relieved to not see a loop of bowel hanging down.

"Can you hold his lead while I give him an intravenous injection?" I asked the woman holding his halter. "Come around to my side of his neck. I don't want him to jump away from me and onto you."

"Sure, he won't spook," she said.

I drew up ten milliliters of the tranquilizer xylazine and walked to the horse's left side. His jugular vein stood out like a blacksnake, and when the drug went in the stud didn't flinch. While he was getting sleepy, I went to the truck for my stainless steel bucket, water, disinfectant, an emasculator, ropes, paper towels, and a few things that I hoped I wouldn't need. Xylazine would make him sleepy, but another drug would be needed to put him on the ground. Getting such a large animal down safely and back up was the hard part. Going down too hard could crack his skull or do other damage.

"I want to give him this other drug, and then I want you to hand me the lead shank and get far away. I want to cushion his head going down, and it will be very sudden," I said, placing the second syringe in the jugular vein. I pushed the plunger, grabbed the lead, and waited.

The big guy started to wobble on legs that were getting less steady and then he began to fall. You don't catch a horse. You try to keep his head from whacking the ground. Down he came, and made a soft landing in the tall grass.

I wrapped a lariat around his right fetlock and pulled his right rear leg toward his neck, wrapping the lariat around a handy tree. This gave me a better look at the area of surgery. "What did you do before you got in trouble?" I asked Robbie.

"I got one seed out and cut it off. The other was harder to reach and then I saw them guts a-pokin' out and quit.

I know my limitations, Doc. That just didn't look right, so I called you."

I washed the blood off the area of the wound and was pleased to see one incision and one testicle. There really wasn't much wrong here. The tissue that Robbie thought might be intestines was only the normal stuff in the scrotum. There wasn't much blood, considering the gallons this horse could lose before he would get into trouble. The incision was in the right place. Robbie was half done, but at least he quit before he (or the horse) got hurt. I scrubbed the stallion's scrotum with disinfectant by the light of the moon and a couple of lanterns. In five minutes I had finished the castration. I gave him an injection of antibiotic and waited for him to wake up.

It's best to let a sleeping horse lie. If you attempt to get one up before the anesthesia has worn off, you can have a staggering, frightened, and uncontrollable horse on your hands. I put my cap over his eye to keep out the lantern light and passed the time putting away instruments.

"I think your horse will be fine," I said to the owner. "I can't believe how lucky you are that no one was hurt," was as close to a lecture as I could give her. Her daughter would remind her of this often enough. I didn't say a lot to Robbie. There was no need.

The big horse got his front feet out in front of him and then lifted his back half.. "Hold his halter to steady him until he's ready to walk back to the barn," I said, handing the lead rope to the owner.

The Indians were ahead by a run as I tuned in the game

on the truck radio. Robbie came up to the window with a sheepish look on his face. "Thanks for helping me out, Doc. I see where I went wrong now. If you need any help gelding stallions, call me. I got the first part down pat."

Emergency!

I'm sitting at my desk in an empty office, waiting for a dog that has been hit by a car. This is something every veterinarian sees much too often. During the summer our small office will average an animal a day hit by a car. These are the ones who live long enough to be brought in, not the number hit. An abbreviation known to veterinarians from Maine to Hawaii is HBC (Hit By Car). It is written in the record, spoken as if it were a word, and universally accepted as an emergency. Since I live close to my office, I can usually arrive before the HBC and have some things prepared.

On this occasion I'm prepared, and awaiting the arrival of "Willard" Jenkins, who climbed over the fence in his backyard to chase a female dog in heat that happened to be passing by. He couldn't resist. A car racing through his neighborhood hit him and rolled him a few times. His owners found him, and should be here with him in the next few minutes. In the meantime, I have a few recollections of emergencies that I'll relate as I wait.

It was Sunday afternoon and I was in the garage packing grease into the front wheel bearings of a 1963 Triumph motorcycle when the phone rang. I wiped the grease from my hands and answered. "Hello."

"Dr. Sharp, this is Evelyn Thomas and I hate to bother

you on Sunday, but we have a calf that my husband tells me has a hemorrhaging tumor on the upper left quadrant of its anus. Can you come and try to save him? It's an emergency."

"Of course, Mrs. Thomas, I'll be right down." Mrs. Thomas was a retired florist and Mr. Thomas a retired electrical engineer. They moved here from the city after buying a small farm, and had beautiful gardens and a few beef steers.

I dropped everything and hit the road. I had a fifteen-mile drive to Harriett Road, and a little farther yet. If the calf were indeed hemorrhaging, I'd better hurry. The three requirements to practice in the country, as told to me by another veterinarian in the area, are to be able to drive a truck like a maniac, rope cattle in the dark, and drive a truck like a maniac. I was learning number two. I had mastered the others.

I pulled into the gravel lane and raised a cloud of dust behind me as I pushed the accelerator hard. I skidded to a stop, jumped out of the truck, grabbed my lariat, and said, "Where is he?"

"Up at the other place. Follow me," said Mr. Thomas as he jumped into his truck.

I didn't know there was another place. I was glad someone had stayed home to meet me. I followed Mr. Thomas, who must have been learning to be a veterinarian since he could already drive like a maniac, and knew enough to say "upper left quadrant of the anus."

We pulled into a lane four miles from their house and raised another cloud of dust speeding up it. I jumped out, lariat in hand, and headed toward Mrs. Thomas, who was standing in the woods. "He's right here!" I thought that if I could catch him, I could cauterize his wound with chemicals, and then decide if the tumor were a surgical problem or if something else would need to be done. Stopping the bleeding was first—after catching him.

Five large calves were in the woods. Each weighed about eight hundred pounds and all were Black Angus crosses. The craziest of calves. Mrs. Thomas knew the one we wanted, so I gradually approached and got my rope ready. I had the Thomases stay back so they wouldn't spook the group. I didn't want a bleeding steer to run away with his blood pressure climbing. The calves turned their backs toward me and started to walk away, so I threw the lariat, and for the first time in history, got the right calf on the first throw. Rodeo Rob.

The calf started to run, so I wrapped the rope around a small maple tree and held on. Three turns around the tree and the calf was mine. I pulled him up closer to the tree, tied the rope, and prepared to view the tumor.

"It's on the upper left quadrant of the anus," repeated Mrs. Thomas.

I eased my way around to the back of the calf and grabbed his tail. I lifted it and said to Mrs. Thomas, "Is this where you saw the problem?"

"Yes, right there it is. You can see it plainly!"

I reached up and knocked a piece of dried cow manure the size of an apple off the hair in the upper left quadrant of the calf's anus. I had successfully performed an emergency "poopectomy."

"Oh, thank God!" said the retired florist.

How do you charge for such a service?

Everyone has a different idea of what constitutes an emergency. When I leave the office in the evening, I leave a message on the answering machine with my home phone number, to be used if a client has an emergency. I get several calls every night, and quite a few more on the days that we aren't open. They all begin the same way. "Dr. Sharp, I hate to bother you at home, but. . . . " From there the story changes. ". . . my dog has had diarrhea for a week, but tonight it's real bad." Or " . . . we just went out to feed Ralph and his collar has grown into his neck." Or the most frequent " . . . my dog's been hit by a car."

I consider an emergency to be whatever the owner of the animal considers an emergency, since I can't see the problem over the phone. If it's an emergency to him or her, it's an emergency to me. Unless it's obviously not. The trick is to know the difference. The reverse is also true. Sometimes an emergency isn't obvious to the owner who just wants a little advice.

One evening, as I was sitting on our screened-in porch watching nothing in particular, the phone rang. I picked up the wireless handset I always have nearby, and said the usual, "Hello."

"Doc, this is Brent Wallis and I hate to bother you at home, but my dog was in a fight and just came up on the porch. I don't think he's hurt too bad, but he has a little blood around his eye. Is there something I can put on it here without bringing him to the office?"

"Where's the blood coming from? Is it from the eye, or the lid?"

"Can't tell. It's not running down his face or anything. My wife has some eye drops that her doctor gave her. Can I just put those in it?"

"What kind of dog do you have?" I asked.

"He's just a little dog that we've had for a while. Maybe a Peek-a-Poo?"

"They have eyes that are accident-prone, since they stick out pretty far. Can you see a scratch?"

"Nope, just a little blood all around it."

"I don't think you ought to put anything in it until I see it. How far do you live from the office?"

"About ten minutes away, but I hate to bother you."

"It's OK. I'll see you in ten minutes."

When Mr. Wallis brought his dog to the office, it was obvious that a little more than a scratch was wrong with his eye. The other combatant had literally knocked this dog's eye out. His eyeball was out of its orbit, or "socket." His eyelids were slammed shut behind the eye. The eye was drying out rapidly since the dog couldn't blink. The optic nerve and vessels were being stretched into submission as a blood clot formed behind the dog's eye. Most people wouldn't even want to look at this mess, let alone think that it just needs eye drops. In a very short time, the eye would have been a dried-up little raisin of a mistake. Oh yes, and there was a little blood around the eye.

I gave the dog an anesthetic, replaced his eye, and sutured the lids closed, asking his owner to bring him back several days later.

When I removed the sutures, the dog's eye was sighted and doing very well. Lucky dog. Unconscious owner.

One day, a very good friend came to the front counter of the office and said, "Rob, Cheesebreath has a tumor on her nose that Bill and I just noticed. I know that cats can get some really bad malignancies and I rushed her right in to you. Can you take a look?"

"Let's see," I said, pulling Cheesebreath out of her carrier. I looked at her nose, took a tissue, and wiped a dried piece of cat food from her snoot. (No, it was not in the upper left quadrant of the nostril.) Did I mention that Cheesebreath's owner was a physician?

A car just pulled into the parking lot. I think tonight's HBC has arrived. I can see out of the office's front window that Willard is walking toward the door with a leg held in the air, but walking on his own. I'm hoping he's just a little bruised and has some road rash. While I was waiting, the phone rang and it was the county recorder's wife, whose dog just fell down the cellar stairs. They'll be here in fifteen minutes with tonight's next emergency. Got to stop now. Willard's here.

Both Ends
of the Lead

I was examining a puppy with skin lesions that belonged to a girl in jeans and a tube top.

"Have these spots been on Bubby since you got him?" I asked.

"Yes, but they're getting worse now. He only had one spot a couple of weeks ago. Now they're everywhere. The hair is coming out in patches all over his back."

It was indeed. It looked like a dermatophyte—a bad case of ringworm. "This is a fairly typical case of ringworm," I advised, " and it's contagious to other dogs and cats as well as humans."

"People can get this?"

"Yes."

"Is this it?" she said, pulling her tube top up to her neck and displaying a fairly typical circular lesion on her right breast.

I'm not usually at a loss for words. The best I could come up with was, "It looks like it to me."

Anyone who thinks a veterinarian solves animal problems, and that the person who accompanies an animal to the office is a minor player, needs to read on. In these stories the owners are as interesting as the bizarre animal problems they present. I think these stories, as a group, might be my favorite ones too. Recalling them for you was a lot of fun, and I hope they give you a feel for treating "both ends of the lead."

The Man from MARS and the Tar Baby

Mr. Gleeson lived in a small trailer at the lake. He was ninety-three years old, independent, and mentally as sharp as when he was twenty. He loved his cats and he had twelve of them to keep him company. When he traveled, they all went with him in his vintage Volkswagen microbus camper.

My aunt Annie would have called him a "long drink of water" and in the winter he liked to wear a black-and-red plaid flannel ball cap with ear flaps swinging loose. He was bright, witty, opinionated, kind, interesting, wise, and soft-spoken. He flew Piper Cubs off the coast of Florida in World War II as a submarine hunter and he still loved flying and the military. He was an active member of the Military Affiliate Radio System (MARS). This network of ham radio operators pass messages daily from military personnel overseas to loved ones in the states. During the Vietnam War I used and appreciated the MARS network when I phoned home to talk to my wife, Susie. Mr. Gleeson was on the air even then, and may have passed my calls home. He sat at his kitchen-table radio station and worked the "waves" for over fifty years, probably with a cat on his lap most of the time. He was a widower but was never alone.

One of Mr. Gleeson's favorite cats was a long-haired, gray-and-white fatso named Gray Lady. She weighed almost eighteen pounds and liked to lie in the sunny spots on the trailer floor. When Mr. Gleeson went outside, so did Gray Lady. Unless of course she had to walk too far. If it looked like a long walk was happening, she would roll over in the sun and wait by the trailer. She was a retired athlete not prone to heavy exercise.

One afternoon in July, it was hot and busy at the office when the microbus unexpectedly pulled into the parking lot. Mr. Gleeson jumped out of the driver's side like it was on fire and ran to the passenger door. "He better slow down or he's gonna have a heart attack!" Melissa, my technician, said. He grabbed a cat carrier, ran to the front door, and burst through.

Out of breath, he said, "It's Gray Lady! I've had a terrible accident! She's covered in silver paint!"

Rhythmic, loud, guttural meowing accompanied his announcement. Gray Lady was very upset and it was obvious. I looked into the carrier and was horrified. A mass of silver-colored tar was painting the inside of the carrier. No cat could be seen, just screaming silver goo. Her eyeballs were the only recognizable part of her, and they were spotted silver.

"I was putting aluminum roof coating on my trailer. I was on top of a stepladder dipping my broom into a five-gallon bucket of the stuff that I had placed on top of another stepladder, when I knocked it off." (Did I mention that he was independent?) "It fell, upside down, right onto Gray Lady."

I had just met the Tar Baby. This stuff is not latex paint. It doesn't come off with water. Just the opposite. It's a petroleum distillate, with aluminum and fibers added so it will stick to a roof and help it repel water. Not only would it not come off Gray Lady, it wouldn't come off anything she touched. The clients in the waiting room were about to find out why a schedule of appointments is not always easy to follow.

"You're going to have to put her to sleep," said Michelle, a high school student who worked at the office after school. "She's going to die anyway!"

"Not yet. Take five dollars out of the drawer and go up to the auto parts store by the high school and get some hand cleaner that takes off paint as well as grease."

The screaming in the carrier intensified. One thing was certain, she would need an anesthetic to be handled. She was miserable. The fumes in the carrier alone were going to kill her, and we couldn't allow her to get loose; she would paint the office silver. I identified her south end and gave a her quick injection of an anesthetic. Slowly the serenade became softer, and then silent.

Michelle returned with a hand cleaner cream. "Let's take her outside on a blanket and try the hand cleaner out there. We can rinse it off with the hose," I said.

It didn't work. The tar won. We now had a slimy, cream-covered, silver tar baby. I did rinse her eyes with artificial tears and put protective eye lubricant in them.

"There is one thing that might work," I said. "Wrap the clippers in bandage material so we don't ruin them. We're going to clip off the hair and tar together. Maybe the hand cream will work better on skin."

I went back to the scheduled appointments while

Melissa clipped Gray Lady. "How much should I clip?" she said.

"Every last hair—whiskers to tail hair—everything silver."

I checked her progress after each appointment and it seemed to be working. Each pass of the clipper would take off more tar-soaked hair. After half an hour Gray Lady was naked. It's a good thing she was asleep too. If she could have seen herself, she would have run away. Fat rolls and a rat tail are a long way from the elegant, long-haired feline we were used to seeing. She was definitely incognito. We took her into the office, put her in the big sink, and went to work with the hand cleaner and water. This time we were winning. The last traces of silver disappeared. We ruined two clipper blades, a wraparound lab coat, four towels, a blanket, a pair of pants, and a watchband in the process.

"We'd better put her in the incubator to wake up. I think she's going to be a little chilly."

We kept her in the incubator for three days as she gradually started to eat and act normal. Mr. Gleeson was thrilled with her progress and visited daily. She had developed a corneal ulcer that responded nicely to treatment, and now there was no reason to keep her.

A week later, Mr. Gleeson brought her back for a visit. She had stubble growing everywhere and was 100 percent normal. He gave us a box of candy in appreciation and said that because of her recent ordeal he had given her a new name: Silver Queen.

For the next several years I always thought I could see a hint of silver in Silver Queen's hair. She probably lost one of her nine lives but became famous at our practice in doing so. I'm reminded of her and Mr. Gleeson when I buy my favorite fall sweet corn, Silver Queen.

Mr. Gleeson's kitchen-table radio station is off the air now. One day he didn't feel well and called his daughter in a town an hour away. When she got to Hillsboro to take him to the doctor, she found him dead in his favorite chair, surrounded by his favorite things. His trailer was sold, and his cats went to live with his daughter. No mention of his death appeared in the paper. He was a patriot, a cat lover, and a friend, and I'll miss him. He was the anonymous radio operator who gave the soldiers in three wars a little bit of home by making radio contact with loved ones. He was not anonymous to me.

Brownie

Marian Nelson taught in a one-room schoolhouse throughout her entire career. The little school in Paint Valley below Rainsboro had educated all of the local farm kids since before the turn of the century. Consolidation, modernization, and time caught up with her and retirement was the natural outcome. She watched her last flock of kids move on to junior high and went home to stay.

She lived in the same beautiful hills where she had taught, raising a few calves, chickens, goats, and a couple of farm dogs. Students had been her life. She had never married and her dogs had become the new focus of her attention. They were her family. They were her friends.

Retired teachers don't make a lot of money but her dogs were always well cared for. Brownie, a thirty-pound dog of mixed heritage, was her constant companion. When she came to town to buy groceries, Brownie was in the backseat. They were always seen together.

Age and isolation can blunt the edges of a previously sharp mind and Miss Nelson became "eccentric." When Brownie became pregnant, Miss Nelson kept the pups. They all looked like their mom, and since it was hard to distinguish one from another, she naturally called them all Brownie. She built elaborate pens next to the barn, complete with a doghouse for each. Nature and time provided her with more companions, and by the time parvovirus reared its devastating head in 1980, there were twenty-eight Brownies living on the farm with the retired teacher.

Parvovirus can kill a dog in less than twenty-four hours. When the national outbreak occurred, vaccines were in their infancy, and dogs died in terrifying numbers. Every day we saw new cases. Bloody diarrhea and vomiting preceded death, except in pups that were very young. They would die suddenly from cardiac complications without much warning that they were even sick. The laundry room at the office became an isolation ward and was filled with dogs on intravenous fluids. Some, older dogs with exceptional immune systems, would survive. The majority would die despite treatment.

Drug companies worked day and night to produce vaccines that would protect against this new plague. Vaccination in advance of exposure was the solution, but the vaccines only trickled into the office. The national demand was huge. Every dog in America was at risk and the vaccine distributors could not keep up.

Miss Nelson came into the office on a warm August morning in 1980 with a worrisome announcement. "Dr. Sharp. Brownie has diarrhea and there's a lot of blood in it!"

"Bring her in and let's take a look," I said, looking out at the old Buick with three dogs in it. I wondered if Brownie singular or plural had diarrhea. If this were parvovirus, she could have her own epidemic and lose them all.

The dog's stool sample looked like currant jelly and the white blood cell count was almost nonexistent. Definitely parvovirus. "Miss Nelson, how many dogs are sick?" I asked.

"Just this one. The others seem fine."

"Have any of the dogs been vaccinated?"

"Oh no. You can't touch most of them. They don't like to be handled, you know. I just feed them and clean up after them."

"If we don't vaccinate them quickly, they will all have this. This is a really contagious virus and some of your dogs have already been exposed. I'll go out to the car and vaccinate the other two dogs while you help Melissa fill out records on them."

Arrangements were made for me to go to the farm that evening after work and vaccinate the other twenty-five dogs. It would take almost all of the vaccine in the refrigerator, but more was expected soon. I looked down at the two new records. Both dogs were named Brownie.

Treatment was begun on Brownie the Sick. I thought about the upcoming trip to her farm all afternoon, and decided that catching and holding twenty-five wild dogs might require an assistant. Dr. Bill Lukhart was the logical choice since he was always up for anything. When I bought his practice he'd said, "Rob, if you need help, you know my number."

This was a man who had once climbed a water tower to take a swim. This was a man who, as a kid, brought a sick camel home from the circus for his father to treat. This was a man who carried the sloshing severed head of a horse in a washtub across the Ohio State University campus in order to have a rabies test done quickly. This was the man for me. The Great Dog Roundup was a two-man job, and Bill was fearless. He, of course, agreed.

On the trip to Miss Nelson's farm, we talked about possible methods of dealing with the dogs. In the truck we had slip leashes, a lariat, a capture pole, and all the equipment used for large-animal cases. Our plan was to chase a dog into a corner, slip a leash over its head for control, and stick it with the shot. One man catching, one giving shots. It sounded so easy in the truck.

Our destination was the third house on the left past the empty school. It was a white frame farmhouse with an old weathered barn out back. They'd both probably looked better ten years earlier when Miss Nelson was better able to care for the place. She greeted us as we pulled in. "I'm glad to see that you brought help. I was worried about how we'd do this. Some of these dogs are not used to strangers." It was hard to hear over the barking and growling of twenty-five dogs.

Pens had been constructed out of chain-link fence, chicken wire, wooden boards, packing boxes, barn parts, anything handy. Growing around the barn were gardens of beautiful flowers, but growing in and out of the warren of dog pens was multiflora rose. This is weed of a rose that can best be described as a thicket of thorns—a briar patch. The dogs had worn pathways and tunnels through this stuff, and now had the advantage. There were three dogs, three doghouses, and fifty thousand thorns in each pen.

"This could be tricky," Bill said. No argument.

I prepared three doses of vaccine, adding the contents of

their attached diluent bottles to the three bottles of freeze-dried vaccine virus. Loading the syringes and holding them at the ready, I said, "Do you want to catch or stick?"

"I'll catch the first three. We'll perfect our technique on them."

One hour later our technique was still being perfected. We had vaccinated two of the first three. Two dogs would run into a single doghouse, and while we tried to snare one inside, the third would come behind us to bite our nonmoving parts. We decided that one of us would be the defensive vet, and one would go on offense. Miss Nelson was the cheerleader outside the fence saying "Now Brownie, you be nice," over and over.

Catching a dog in the briar patch was out of the question and the dogs soon learned this was the "safe area." Back and forth they went, snarling, dodging, snapping, and I think, laughing. We took a break.

"What are we doing wrong?"

"First," Bill said, "we're going to mix all the vaccine and put it in a cattle gun so we can poke, squeeze the trigger, and vaccinate with one hand. Next, we're being too fussy in our injection-site location. Poke the dog, anywhere on the dog. Third, let's send Marian to the house to make lemonade. I've had about all the 'now Brownies' I can stand." Wise words.

We mixed twenty doses of vaccine, loaded it in a pistol syringe, and asked for lemonade. Miss Nelson didn't have lemonade, and so Bill suggested that she go to the Carmel general store just up the road while we continued our work. I gave her five dollars, and phase two was complete.

We added new weapons to our side in the battle—garbage-can lids.

ROBERT T. SHARP, DVM

We entered the briar-filled coliseum like a pair of gladiators, shield in one hand, pistol syringe in the other. Bill would herd one Brownie toward me; I would push it to the ground and vaccinate it with one move. Occasionally I missed and we repeated the process. We finished in an hour and used thirty-four doses to vaccinate twenty-five dogs. Neither of us was bitten and every dog was treated. Success.

At sundown Miss Nelson returned with lemonade. They didn't have any at the Carmel store, so she'd driven into Hillsboro, twenty-two miles away.

The epidemic continued that summer. Many dogs died but Miss Nelson never lost a single one. Bill and I had gone back three weeks later and given them the necessary boosters. Brownie, singular and plural, was fine.

Years passed, Miss Nelson's mind deteriorated, and eventually the court appointed a guardian for her. The humane society took charge of the Brownies, and Miss Nelson was without an animal friend.

She still lived at home with round-the-clock caregivers, and as her condition continued to worsen, everyone agreed that her outlook might improve if she had a pet. A small dog was selected. The guardian called our office to make an appointment.

I walked into the exam room and shook hands with her guardian, and attorney, Jim Harper. I thought the caregiver's selection was perfect. There on the table was a small, mixed breed, brown-and-white dog. I said, "Well, the one thing I'm sure of is what Miss Nelson will name her."

Mr. Harper said, "She was certain too. We took the pup to her bedside and placed it on the bed. She lit up like it was Christmas and tears came to her eyes. Without any hesitation she said, 'Come here, Whitey!'"

Gratitude

Gerald Maxwell was an arrogant chap. He liked that word, "chap." Though he was born and reared in a county where people thought of "chap" as the condition of the teats on a dairy cow in December or someone's lips after a hot date, Gerald used it all his life to describe people. "A fine chap."

In addition to being arrogant, he was rich and wanted only the best of everything. His parents had told him as a child that he wasn't like everyone else and I guess he believed it. He put on a good show, anyway. He could invigorate a tired waitress with anger when he snapped his finger and shouted "girl" across a restaurant full of people to get her attention. He was seventy-five years old and had not yet been hit by a plateful of eggs. Shirred, of course, Dear, not over easy.

When Gerald and his wife, Matilda, decided to get a dog, it couldn't be a mutt. Common people have mutts. They studied the AKC Dog Book and decided that a Tibetan terrier would be just right for them. They had never seen one and neither had any of their friends. They weren't concerned with things like temperament or conformation. Just so it was different. They found a breeder with an adult male that had been returned for undisclosed reasons and decided that he would be "perfect." It didn't matter that he was nuts.

Thunder was a bad dog. He was willful, untrained, undisciplined, and would bite anyone who tried to touch him. Gerald and Matilda thought that this was the way all dogs acted, since they'd never owned a dog in all their lives. "He was a fine chap, just a tad rowdy."

Most dogs, like most people, are easy to get along with. But just as with people, there are insane dogs, ill-tempered dogs, and dogs that can only be described as criminal. Thunder was one of these. Unpredictable and mean, he had no redeeming qualities.

Thunder did do some things right. He allowed Gerald to feed him. He allowed Gerald to walk him. He allowed Gerald to pet him. Every morning and evening Gerald could be seen walking Thunder. In a town where bib overalls and ball caps are the uniform of the day, Gerald preferred to wear a smoking jacket and ascot while walking his dog. To anyone who didn't know Thunder, he looked like a great pet. He presented the perfect picture of canine companionship, and Gerald was very loyal to him.

Every year my examination of Thunder was cursory at best. He could never be placed on the exam table, and listening to his heart or lungs with a stethoscope was impossible. He growled constantly, unless he was trying to bite. "He must not like you, Doc," or "He must smell other dogs in here. You know he doesn't like other dogs," or "He's a bit upset today since he didn't get his morning walk," or "He doesn't like those scales." Every possible excuse. Neither Gerald nor Matilda could hold his leash reliably. Thunder knew this. He was a good chap, just a bit rowdy.

Once, when he was six years old, Thunder apparently had pneumonia. I say "apparently" because determining this was impossible. He wouldn't allow a stethoscope near him. He couldn't be muzzled because a muzzle would restrict his breathing. Blood couldn't be drawn without extreme restraint, and tranquilizers might be dangerous since he was breathing with difficulty anyway. Anyone's approach caused him to snarl and snap. He was sent home with antibiotics which Gerald couldn't administer, and so, once daily, he was brought to the office for a shot. He lived.

A week later, I saw Gerald and Thunder on their usual morning jaunt. Thunder was a good chap, just a bit rowdy.

One day the Maxwells' big red Cadillac pulled into the parking lot and Matilda came in asking to speak with me in private. "Dr. Sharp, would it be terrible of me to ask you to put Thunder to sleep? You know he's bitten Gerald several times and I don't want my husband to be hurt. Last night, after dinner, Thunder was sleeping in the hallway and Gerald wanted to go to bed. He walked down the hall and when he stepped over Thunder he was bitten on the leg. I can't stand to see him bitten again, but he'll never say anything. You know he loves that dog."

"Are you sure you want to do this? Won't Gerald be really mad at us?" I asked. "Maybe you two should talk it over first."

"I can deal with Gerald. He might be mad, but I won't permit him to keep a dog that bites him. I've never liked that dog and always thought he was mean, but I didn't think he would bite a man who loves him so much. This was the last straw."

"Why don't you bring him over just before lunch and I'll put him to sleep. We can call the funeral home and have his body cremated. That way Gerald won't have to bury him."

This was one case where we would make certain that a euthanasia permission slip was signed. If there was a problem with Gerald, I could show him his wife's signature giving permission for euthanasia. We always do this but there would be no slipup this time. Trouble was brewing.

At noon I put Thunder to sleep and called the funeral home. They picked up his body and my job was done. Forms signed, dog delivered.

The next day I looked out of the exam-room window and saw Gerald driving the big red Caddy into the parking lot at high speed. Trouble was here.

"Put Gerald in a private room and get me that permission slip," I said to Melissa. "I'll go in with him when I finish with the cat in here." I nervously finished vaccinating the cat on the exam table, all the while rehearsing my song and dance in my head.

I opened the door and walked in to meet Gerald.

"Here, Doc," he greeted me holding out a brown bag.

I looked in the bag and didn't understand. It was a large bottle of Lynchburg, Tennessee's finest. A bottle of Jack Daniel's.

"I don't understand, Gerald. What's this for?"

"For putting me out of my misery. I've hated that son of a bitch since the day we met. I only put up with him because Matilda loved him so. Thanks so much, Doc. You're a good chap."

What's in a Name?

Mr. and Mrs. Long loved their Dobermans. They'd retired, moved from the city to twelve acres of woods, and bought a registered pair with the intention of raising and selling pups. When the six pups were born, each was immediately named. This was bad. If it's your intention to sell puppies, it's much harder to give up a pup with a name. They found this to be the case, and as a result, eventually they owned eight beautiful dogs that played in their woods.

Each dog developed a unique personality, but they all looked alike. The Longs could tell them apart because of their behavior and a few different facial expressions, but every time I entered the exam room and saw Mr. Long with a Dobe sitting next to him, I was never sure if it was Sundance, who loved me, or Moonlight, who hated everyone, or Moonbeam, who would wag his little tail before attacking. Skylark was a face-licker. Rainbow was a heel-biter. Starfire froze to the floor at the sight of strangers, and so on and so forth.

It was Russian roulette. I had notes on each dog's idiosyncrasies written in its record. Making a mistake could be bad news. Painful too. If Mr. Long brought three or four dogs in at once, he would leave some in the car while I examined one at a time. Let's see, who did he say this was? I would think to myself.

Over the years I had my favorites and I even got pretty good at telling the members of the Doberman Gang apart. One thing I knew for certain: The Longs would never be robbed.

Nothing good can last forever, and Prince was the first to die. He developed spinal cord problems that were both painful and debilitating. He was the patriarch, and difficult for the Longs to give up. The day we euthanized him was a sad one for us all. But as time went on, we lost the rest one by one to a variety of different accidents and illnesses. The youngest to die was Sundance at nine years. The oldest was Thunder at thirteen. The Longs were also aging, and a year after Thunder died, Mrs. Long was hospitalized and passed away.

On the way home from his wife's funeral service in Cincinnati, Mr. Long decided that he was unable to go home to an empty house. He missed the fun they had enjoyed with the Doberman Gang. He stopped at the Clermont County Animal Shelter and went inside.

"Do you ever have any Dobermans that need a home?" he asked the volunteer behind the counter.

"Let me look at our current list," she said. "Looks like we don't have one now and to tell you the truth, I can't remember the last time we had one. They are not very often strays or given away."

Just then the woman standing behind him said "Are you looking for a Dobe?"

"Sure am. Do you have one?"

"As a matter of fact I do. My mother just died and we can't take her dog. We have a rottweiler and they would fight until one was killed. This is a male and he's a big guy. I really didn't want to bring him here but have no choice. I've got him out in the car."

"I've had a lot of Dobes over the years and I'd be glad to make a good home for him," said Mr. Long anxiously.

They met in the parking lot and it was love at first sight. Mr. Long was no longer saturated with grief. He had company on the trip home.

The next day he brought Majestic in to see me.

"I was sorry to hear about Mrs. Long's death," I said clumsily. "Where did you get Majestic?"

"You'll never believe it, Doc! Just when I thought things were going down the tubes, a woman with a dog saved me. They didn't have any Dobes at the shelter, and like she was sent from Heaven, this woman showed up. She came in right behind me to drop off Majestic. I couldn't believe it!"

"You just got him yesterday?"

"On the way home from the funeral. Isn't he great? They said they rarely get Dobes there, too."

"He's really a handsome guy. Did she give you any

paperwork with him, like a shot record? We ought to see when his shots will be due."

"She did." He handed me a stack of papers.

"Honest to God, Doc, I'd never been so depressed. The thought of going home was terrible, and now I have Majestic. He really was a gift from God. Of course, he doesn't know his name yet. I called him Majestic but she called him something stupid like Divin."

I looked through his vaccination history and found his name. It immediately gave me the willies. The big red Dobe in front of me was registered with the AKC as "Divine Intervention."

"I can't believe this, Bob. His name is Divine Intervention. He really is a gift from God!"

Without looking up, or a moment's hesitation, he said, "I think I'll call him Majestic. I like it better."

Bathing Beauty

I jumped when the phone rang. Five years as a navigator in the Strategic Air Command of the US Air Force had conditioned me like one of Pavlov's dogs. I spent one week out of three running to an airplane at the sound of a klaxon. A phone call at midnight always has the same effect on me; I woke up and was running to the plane when I realized it was only the telephone.

"Is this the vitnary?"

"Whom were you calling?" I asked, hoping he wanted a Mr. Vitnary.

"The vitnary. The vitnary. The dog doctor."

"This is Dr. Sharp," I admitted.

"Thank God, Doc. This is Elmont Sunbeam and I've got a real problem here. My dog's got a tumor."

"Is this an emergency tumor?" I asked, wondering why he was calling at midnight for a problem that had probably been going on for weeks or months. Tumors don't develop instantly. But once discovered, they always require instant treatment.

"I was just bathing Beauty and there it was."

I didn't ask why he was giving a bath to a dog at midnight. Some people work different shifts and have strange habits. "Is it bleeding?"

"No."

"Is it draining fluid or does it smell bad?"

"No."

"Do you think this is something that can wait 'til morning?"

"Oh, I don't know, Doc. It's real ugly and my wife is real worried about it."

"I'll come in tonight to see it if you don't think it can wait. Of course I charge more for a night call."

"I think it can wait 'til morning, but will you see it first thing?" I went back to sleep wondering what the tumor would look like. I did know Beauty would be looking good. She had just had a midnight bath.

The next day arrived all too soon, and as I had breakfast, I wondered what I'd told the Sunbeams to do the night before. When you're awakened out of a sound sleep and given a quiz by the caller, your answers may not be the same ones you'd give someone when you're not half asleep. When I got to the office, I expected them to be waiting at the door. They were. I pulled my truck around to the back, went inside, took off my coat, put on a lab coat, and went to the exam room. Melissa had placed the Sunbeams in the room already. I opened the door, said "good morning," and was immediately struck by the contrast in body shapes sitting next to one another. Mrs. Sunbeam was a spherical woman of great size. The bangs of her hairdo cut across her huge face like the lid of a jack-o-lantern. She wore tiny dark glasses that cut into her temples, and she carried a white cane with a red tip. Mr. Sunbeam was a shriveled, dried-out little prune of a man whose overalls hung from his shoulders and collected at his feet. He must have been taller and heavier once. He was the eyes of the association, but definitely not in charge. Next to them sat a beautiful female German shepherd.

"Show him the tumor, Jack. He hasn't got all day. Put Beauty on the table. Show him that tumor you found. Just lift her up on that table."

"It really isn't necessary to lift . . ." I started to say.

"Hurry up, Jack, put her up there . . ."

As the hundred-pound man tried to lift the eighty-pound dog, I grabbed a few of the dog's body parts to help. She landed on the exam table a little awkwardly.

I put my hand on Beauty's head and gave her a little pat, just to let her know it was over. She gave me a look that I interpreted as the look of experience. Ungraceful landings were obviously routine with the Sunbeams.

I examine every dog in the same sequence, starting at the tip of the nose and working my way back. I made it to the eyes. Using an ophthalmoscope I had begun to look at Beauty's left eye when Mrs. Sunbeam couldn't keep quiet any longer. "What's he doing, Jack? Has he seen the tumor yet? What's it look like, Doc?"

"I'm just giving her my usual examination, Mrs. Sunbeam.

You never know what you'll find if you don't look. Right now I'm looking in her eyes."

"Her eyes ain't the problem. It's the other end. Jack says it's near her private parts. Show him, Jack. Don't just stand there. He's a busy man. Help him find it."

Mrs. Sunbeam didn't like to waste time.

I moved straight to the south end of the dog, not wanting Jack to be in trouble for something that was obviously my fault. I found no tumor. I ran my hands all over the dog and found no tumor. Finally I asked Jack for help. "Can you point it out? I'm having a little trouble finding it."

"It's pretty big and right there by her private parts."

I looked again. We rolled her over. I looked again. Finally I said, "Jack, put your finger on the tumor."

He slowly lowered his finger to the spot.

I knew that what I was about to say would have immediate and predictable results in the Sunbeam household. Like throwing a minnow to a piranha. "Jack, those *are* her private parts."

Prickly Problem

Kids love animals and animals love kids. It's a fact of life. Neither one minds if the other isn't perfect. They love each other in spite of a few flaws. Kids don't care if a dog's not house-trained perfectly or if it eats a priceless heirloom. Dogs don't care if a kid cleans his or her room or doesn't. A perfect pair. Some pairs are a little different.

"Dr. Sharp, there's a little girl in the waiting room who says she won't go back to school in Columbus until you fix her hedgehog," Melissa said, poking her head around the corner from the front office as I was finishing a cat spay. "She doesn't have an appointment, and her parents are outside in the car. Do you want to see her?"

"How can we turn down a kid with a hedgehog? What's the matter with it?"

"She says that it was burrowing in its cage blanket and got a thread wrapped around its leg. Now its foot is twice its normal size."

"That shouldn't take more than thirty seconds to fix. Let me put these last few stitches in Half Tail, and I'll see her. Just put her in the big exam room."

Her parents waited in the car while Jenny brought in her pet.

I finished the surgery, washed my hands, and walked into the exam room. A beautiful little girl with big glasses stood on the far side of the exam table. She was no more than ten years old. "Hi. I'm Dr. Sharp. I hear you have a hedgehog with a leg problem."

She held her little pal in a towel. "I'm Jenny Jaffe and this is Sonic. His foot is really swollen and I think something is wrapped around his leg."

What else could a hedgehog be named but Sonic? Kids always pick the best names for pets, and then adults interrupt the natural process and add their two cents' worth. This is how good names like Spot for a rat terrier with a spot on its back are eventually contorted into the parents' choice of Shania. The kid gets overruled. Here the kid won, and it was obvious.

"Can I see his foot?" I asked.

Jenny put the towel on the table, and as I unwrapped it, I saw a rolled-up ball of thorny spikes, but no foot. Sonic was in the defensive position.

"We think it happened yesterday. No one noticed that his foot was big before that."

"Hey, Jenny, how do we get him to unroll? He's all wrapped up in a ball."

"He's pretty scared. When he gets scared, he rolls up."

I touched him and he jumped, sticking me with a few spines. Obviously a good defense mechanism, but not conducive to examination. "Can we pull him out straight?"

"I don't think so. He's pretty strong. We've never been able to unroll him when he doesn't want to. And he does that jumpy thing when you touch him."

"I noticed." So much for the thirty-second fix. "OK, Sonic, let's try again." I tried to turn him over and he did that jumpy thing again, sticking me in the finger.

"Did he get you?" Jenny asked smiling.

"Yup, he stuck me. What are we gonna do, Jenny? We have to see that foot to fix it. I have to cut the string around the leg."

"Can you give him a shot of something to make him go to sleep?"

"I don't know where to give the shot. His legs are rolled up inside and his back is covered with those spines. That's a good idea though. Maybe we could give him a little gas anesthetic. We just need a little time to get the string off his leg, so he doesn't have to be asleep for long."

"Will it hurt him?" Jenny asked, sensing the apprehension in my voice.

"I've never done this before, but I don't think the anesthetic will do anything unpredictable. We can put him under a glass container and put a cotton ball with a little anesthetic on it in with him. As he begins to get sleepy, we'll get him out of the glass and cut the string on his foot before he wakes up. How's that sound?"

"Let's try it. I really like him and I hope you can fix his foot."

I found a glass container that said "cotton" on the side, and tried to put it over Sonic as he sat rolled up on the exam table. A perfect fit. I found a little gauze and put some liquid isoflurane on it. I put the gauze on the table next to Sonic and covered them both with the glass container.

"What's happening?" Jenny asked.

"Nothing yet, but we're watching."

Within thirty seconds, Sonic started to get relaxed. "He's getting sleepy. Let's try to unroll him." I removed our glass chamber and placed Sonic on his back. He flopped his arms and legs out like a free-fall parachutist. "Boy, he does have a swollen foot. But I can see the string that's caused it. I'm going into the other room for a second to get a few things. I'll be right back."

"I'll be right here," Jenny said.

A very fine thread had been wrapped tightly around the hedgehog's hock, cutting off the circulation to his foot. If it remained there long enough, the foot could become gangrenous. "Let's get this thread off of his leg." I slipped the tip of a pair of suture-cutting scissors under the thread and cut it. Several wraps of thread were removed. "There, that's off. Now let's run warm water on the leg to dilate the crunched blood vessels and get some circulation back in his foot. I'm going into the room across the hall. Want to come?"

"Sure, I'll follow you."

I adjusted the water temperature of the faucet to very warm, and held the little guy's leg under the stream. Jenny was right next to me. As we warmed up Sonic's leg, we talked about her classes in Columbus. She was a very mature and well-spoken little girl. She thought that she might become a teacher when she was older. As the water warmed Sonic's leg, he started to wake up. "He's already awake. I don't think we'll get much 'hydrotherapy' done, but maybe it will be enough."

As soon as Sonic was awake, he rolled back up into the armored-ball position. "I think he'll be fine, but watch that foot for a few days just to make sure that the swelling goes down."

"I'll keep an eye on it," she laughed as she walked to the exit door. "Thanks for fixing Sonic, Dr. Sharp. I really appreciate it."

Interesting little animal. And what a nice kid. I never met her parents, but then I guess I didn't need to. I met Jenny and Sonic. It made no difference to any of us that Jenny was blind.

The Gift

Some sermons are better than others. Even the preacher knows that and can tell you himself which of them he considers uplifting and which sleep inducing. I was listening (sort of) to one of the latter when my wandering eyes saw the back of an unfamiliar head in church. I'm a back-row Presbyterian, since the leg room in the back is better and the view of the congregation happens to be better too. This head was different.

It had shoulder-length, wild brown hair compressed around the middle from years of wearing a ball cap. This hair stack was perched on top of a heavy wool hounds-tooth sport coat, uncomfortable for such a hot summer day. I deduced that we had a visitor who probably had only one Sunday sport coat. His ball-cap line meant he might be a farmer. The fact that he was alone meant he was unmarried, or surely his wife would have accompanied him on this first time in our church. And he must be a devout and faithful Presbyterian to be suffering alone, with such a heavy coat on such a hot day. A potential new member and someone to greet after church.

I was not entirely correct. When the final hymn and benediction were over and I eased out to the aisle to say hello, I thought, Hey, I know that guy!

Full beard, flannel shirt under the sport coat, brown work pants, and (believe it or not) a pair of midcalf rubber farm boots—this was none other than Galen Thompson, of the coon-hunting Thompsons. He and his uncle Fay lived at the edge of the county, maybe twenty miles from town. They raised a few head of cattle, a few hogs, and usually had at least one horse tied to a tree somewhere on the farm. They were both competition coon hunters and also trained a few dogs that could be bought for the right price. The fact that these dogs might be priced at several thousand dollars meant that they could live on the farm in the trunk of a *good* abandoned car. They were, after all, "Registered Spotted Leopard Curs." Registered with whom I do not know.

"Hi, Galen!" I said, holding out my welcome-to-church hand. "I didn't know you were Presbyterian."

"Hi, Doc. I'm not."

"Did you come to check out the minister, or were you just in town and thought you'd try a different denomination?" I couldn't let this go. I really wondered why he was here. Not exactly a "True Christian Attitude."

He leaned in close to me, like a guy with a big secret, and said, "Just checkin' out your women."

That was Galen. Apparently nobody had ever told him that when you're cruisin' for chicks in church, it helps to take off your boots.

Well, a month passed, and Galen called the office with an emergency. Melissa came to the back room where I was paying the monthly bills, and said, "Galen Thompson is on the phone and says they have big trouble. A cow is bloated and nothing he's given her has helped. He needs you right now or she'll die."

Bloat in a beef cow is a serious thing. Something the cow has eaten has fermented in the rumen and the resulting froth and bubbles can't be burped up like normal cow digestive gasses. As a result, the rumen distends until it can't get any bigger, and then the cow usually dies from toxins that accumulate in the blood, or from simple respiratory arrest from extreme pressure. She needed a solution of "antiferment medicine" and she needed it now. Occasionally a trocar (a huge hollow needle as big around as your index finger) is inserted into the rumen to relieve the pressure and allow medicine to be injected.

I grabbed the phone and said, "I'm leaving right now, Galen. I'll be there in about twenty-five minutes."

"Hurry, Doc. She looks like she's gonna blow!"

I drove as fast as I could, knowing that time was truly critical. The road to Peebles was treacherous and hilly but I arrived in the promised twenty-five minutes.

The patient was still standing, and the left side of her abdomen bulged like a balloon squeezed in an elevator door.

She looked like she was indeed "about to blow," and I was almost afraid to get near her. I opened the back of my truck, took out an eight-inch trocar, and walked to the cow's left side. I picked a spot over the rumen that would be my location for insertion. This would be like stabbing a basketball with a kitchen knife and I needed to be sure I was on target. With one overhand plunge, the trocar entered the rumen, and gas started to escape through the needle like a tire going flat. It smelled like grass and methane, and was probably flammable. She deflated over a five-minute period and when she stopped "hissing," I inserted antifermenting medication through the same trocar.

"Will she be OK, Doc?" Galen asked, having watched from the front end of the cow.

"I think so. I'm glad you found her when you did, though. I don't think she would have lasted much longer."

"You ain't a-kiddin', Doc. We had one do this a week ago and she didn't make it. She got so big that Fay got a kitchen knife and was a-gonna de-bloat her like you just did. He stabbed her to let out the gas, but she went ahead and died on us. Course he didn't stab her where you did."

"Where did he stab her, Galen?" I asked, afraid of the answer.

"Over here."

He walked over to the right side of the cow and pointed to a spot between the ninth and tenth ribs. He had stabbed her in the lungs. Probably the cause of death.

"We called you today so's to see how the pros do it. Now I see where we went wrong. Hey Doc, on your way up the lane, stop at the house and I'll give you a present."

I packed my bags in the truck and drove back to the house. Galen was standing in the drive with a package wrapped in white butcher paper. "A little something for you and the family. A couple of steaks."

"Thanks a lot, Galen. Did you raise the beef yourself?"

"Yup. Remember that bloated cow that Fay stabbed? That's her."

I drove back to town smelling the faint odor of methane that must permeate the meat when a cow is bloated. I walked into the back door of the office and was greeted by Melissa. "How'd it go?"

"Pretty well. She'll live. Oh, by the way, Galen sent you some steaks."

Amazing Grace

The headlights of the old car made the fog glow, as two white shafts illuminated the road ahead. It was a cold November night and the all-day rain had slowed to a drizzle. The smell in the station wagon was something that took some getting used to. People who wear heavy perfume find that they can't smell it at all after a while, and splash on even more. Olfactory fatigue. This was no perfume. Seven dogs were in the station wagon, and a thousand pounds of dog food. The dogs had had a few "accidents" and were spreading them around on the newspaper that covered the back compartment. For the old woman at the wheel, who had smelled urine-and fecal-soaked newspapers for years, olfactory fatigue had set in. The windshield wipers slapped a constant cadence as she drove.

She was on her way home from her weekly run into the city. A nice man at a grocery chain store would save all his damaged bags of dog food, and sell them to her at a discount.

A big discount. Some weren't really damaged but were included anyway. He was a dog lover, and knew of her work.

Suddenly, in the headlights, a little girl appeared at the edge of the road. She was no more than eight years old. Then two women and two more kids were visible. An old rusty conversion van was pulled onto the tall grass next to the road. Someone was in trouble and needed help. Of course, there was only one thing to do. Pull over and help.

The unlikely benefactor pulled up behind the van and slowly got out to investigate. Walking up to the women with the help of a cane, the eighty-year-old diabetic great-grandmother said with a shrill, heavy Massachusetts accent, "What are you doing out here on this kind of night? What's wrong? Do you have car trouble?"

Thalia Gorton must have looked a little strange coming out of the fog. The way she was dressed—in a yellow, flowered knit cap that said PEPSI and a bright purple, puffy down coat, her tennis shoes flopping loose on her feet—was a perfect example of function over form. Matching colors, matching styles, or even matching shoes were not a necessity. She was a bent-over, gnomelike little woman with a mammary endowment that gave her constant back problems. Her crackling voice was her most distinctive feature, after her huge heart.

"We're out of gas. Can you take us to a gas station?"

"Well of course, get in my car. Get those kids and your friend in too. They'll be killed out here in the fog. Don't worry about these dogs, they're friendly. Get in! Get in!"

Five miles up the Appalachian Highway, she found a gas station that was open and would loan an old woman a can to hold gas. On the way back to the stranded van, Mrs. Gorton learned that the two women and three little girls were really on their way to nowhere. They were living in the van, and would be spending the night at the roadside rest a few miles up the road.

"God is so gracious! You have nowhere to live and I have a big old house and need some help. Why don't you come stay with me and help me with my dogs? I have a lot of dogs at home and it's hard for me to take care of them by myself. You can stay with me for free. What do you think? You may not know this, but God put us together!"

The two stranded women thought the proposed arrangement sounded good. They needed a place to stay, and feeding dogs sounded easy. So it was settled. Mrs. Gorton had taken in a few more strays.

Her dogs were her life's joy and assignment. People who had heard of her would take dogs to her, and she would have them spayed or neutered and ask for only a small reimbursement in return. People would take litters of pups to her just to get rid of them, and she would worm them, get them shots, love them, and find homes for them. Sometimes, if they were hard to place, they would live with her for the rest of their lives. She was known in the area as "the Dog Lady."

Her home, as you can imagine, was unusual. Her house was on sixty acres of land she called The Haven. Local out-of-work men had built many outdoor pens for the dogs. Many. She lived with and cared for her ninety-nine-year-old senile mother; her husband, who suffered from Parkinson's disease; and at this time, about sixty-five dogs and a houseful of cats. She could use some help.

There was a time when she had had well over a hundred dogs. Each had a name and a history. Many of the dogs were aging now and had been with her for many years. Some had suffered from mange as pups, and had large areas of hair missing. Who would adopt a dog that looked like this? No one, and so they lived with her. She never considered them her own, even though some had been with her for over fifteen years. All were available for adoption, even though the old, the lame, the hairless, and the nondescript had no chance of finding a home. Her county had no animal shelter, and the dog warden shot strays. So Mrs. Gorton provided shelter as well as an eighty-year-old retired woman could manage to do. She couldn't bear to see animals in need.

She had help from a large veterinary practice in the city and a little help from me. Over the last twenty years, she had personally seen to it that more than eight hundred dogs had been spayed, neutered, and vaccinated. Mrs. Gorton would never make an appointment—she preferred to drop in. This was especially exasperating in the middle of the afternoon, when the office was filled with people and I was running behind with scheduled appointments. On the other hand, if she sat in the waiting room, the earthy fragrance of sixty-five dogs and a houseful of cats was overwhelming to those without olfactory fatigue. We had to get her in and out as quickly as possible. As frustrating as she could be, she would always make me laugh with tales of her oddball adventures, and the women in the fog were typical of her wonderful generosity. Once she asked me if she could borrow five hundred dollars. She used the technique effectively employed by all kids, saying "I've already asked Dr. Mike in the city and he gave me five hundred." I gave it to her knowing two things: she probably didn't want it for herself and she would probably pay it back someday. I later found out that she needed a thousand dollars to buy an old trailer for a young couple that had been thrown out of the place they had called home. I was right on both assumptions. But I digress.

Shortly after finding the van people that night, she brought one of her dogs in to see me and told me the story. "Oh, Dr. Sharp. It's a miracle! God is so gracious. The women don't work real hard, but they do help care for the animals and keep my mother company. The little girls are so precious. They love the animals, and of course, the animals love them. Now, please take a look at Cowboy here. He's had this rash for a couple of weeks. What do you think it is?"

Cowboy always growled and snapped when I looked at him. In the past years I had seen literally hundreds of dogs for Mrs. Gorton. Cowboy was the only dog that would bite, and enjoy it, too. He tried to get me on every single visit. "Cowboy's rash is just a little allergy. It'll be easy to control with pills." Cowboy turned his head my way and I moved my hand. He only weighed fifteen pounds, but was the picture of intensity. "How long do you think your houseguests will stay? Are they looking for work in town or are they going to work for you full time?"

"Well, they aren't educated, and they don't seem to be very motivated either. I've spoken with the pastor at the little church that I attend and he's looking for something for them too. We thought they might be able to get a job at the local Wal-Mart."

I didn't see Mrs. Gorton for a few weeks, but just after Christmas (and five minutes before I would be leaving the office), she pulled up with a van full of puppies, unscheduled, of course. She was very apologetic for the late hour, and as I examined and vaccinated her pups, she told a strange tale.

"Do you remember those two women who were living with me?"

"I remember. Are they still helping you with the dogs?"

"No! You won't even believe this! I bought Christmas gifts for all of them. When the little girls were trying on the clothes I bought, I noticed bruises all over their bodies. I asked them what had happened, and they said they fell down. Those women must have been beating the little girls when I wasn't there. So I went to the minister to ask if I should turn them in, and who could we trust, and you know, that kind of stuff. Well, apparently the kids told the women that I had asked about the bruises. The next afternoon, they robbed me, and left. They didn't get much, since I don't have much to steal, but I'm really worried about those little girls. I've told the authorities, but they said they're long gone by now. Did I tell you about the rats?"

"No, what rats," I asked, knowing how she could change subjects twice in one sentence. Sometimes her conversation was hard to follow.

"They're in my kitchen and on the back porch. They like the cat food so now I have another problem. How do I get rid of them without endangering the cats? I can't use poison, or traps. I've thought about this for a long time. I've decided to put out more food and just feed them too. I don't want to hurt the cats. Great rat catchers I'm living with! Those cats all eat too well. Did I tell you that we found homes for all those puppies that Dr. Mike saw last week? All fifteen. God is so gracious. He'll look after the little girls." She rambled, and didn't always pause for a response.

I didn't see her for quite a while after that. Then I found out the reason. On one of her trips home from the city carrying a load of dog food for the dogs that couldn't be adopted, she was in an accident. A car hit her station wagon from behind while she was stopped at a traffic light. She was hospitalized for several weeks.

During her hospitalization, Mrs. Gorton hired a man to feed and clean up after the dogs and cats. (Her husband and mother were cared for by county services during her absence.) The guy she hired to take care of her animals was a lazy, unreliable bum who only did about half of any job. The dogs were fed and watered when he thought about it. The pens were never cleaned. Cleanliness and order went downhill quickly without Mrs. Gorton's loving hand.

Mrs. Gorton's neighbor never liked the attention, traffic, smell, and noise that went with the old woman's animal work. Her place was too close to his, and he wanted her gone. This turn of events appeared to him to be a great opportunity to get rid of the "old bat" once and for all. He called a television news channel in the city and told them about an animal atrocity that was being perpetrated on their doorstep. He said that there was a crazy lady who was neglecting animals, and if they came quickly, they could film it all for the eleven o'clock news.

The news channel brought a humane society officer from the city, and the local sheriff. Mrs. Gorton came home from the hospital and was met by news cameras and law enforcement officers. She was told to sign over the care of her dogs to the humane society of the city or she would go to jail. She also would have to sign a paper saying that she would not keep dogs anymore.

All she'd ever wanted was to find homes for these dogs, and now the city humane society promised to help. Her prayers had been answered. They would help the dogs find homes. God is so gracious. She was happy to sign.

The dogs were rounded up by men in clean white

uniforms and carted off in trucks. Cowboy wasn't about to go with a stranger, so as a hand reached in to grab him, he bit it, leaped for freedom, and ran for the woods at the back of the farm. Some dogs had been cared for by Mrs. Gorton since they'd been pups, and were now arthritic and feeble. She kissed them all good-bye and told them that they would be in good hands.

The good hands killed them all—all but three, which they placed with new owners, and Cowboy. The Haven was replaced by The Holocaust.

A few months later, a national humane publication boasted of a great success in putting a crazy country animal shelter out of business. The city humane society was commended for its work in ending this inhumane animal treatment. I never showed Mrs. Gorton the article, and her response to the whole episode was predictable: "They were doing what they thought was right. Besides, they didn't say I can't have cats."

In the years that I have known her, she has cared for the animals that no one else would care for: the homeless, ugly, hairless, infirm, crippled, and parasite-laden mutts that roam her county in huge numbers. Cowboy is still with her, and to this day is the only dog she ever had that would bite someone. He owes his life to that quirk.

While Mrs. Gorton is never on time for the appointments she never makes, and can sometimes make the blood pressure of a slug rise, she is a client for whom I would do almost anything. Almost.

When I get frustrated or upset with her, I think of it as a test. I remember the famous quotation from Hebrews 13:2:

Be not forgetful to entertain strangers: for thereby some have entertained angels unawares.

Once in a Lifetime

As a kid I wanted to fly fighters in the Air Force. I'd stay up late so I could watch the television channels sign off with the national anthem. Flying through the clouds, as the Stars and Stripes waved in the background was a jet doing an aileron roll into the sunset. Who wouldn't want a job like that? Sign me up! I want to do aileron rolls into the sunset.

After five years in the Air Force I learned that not every job is as it seems—not all aileron rolls. That includes veterinary medicine. A lot of routine procedures have to be done that aren't quite as glamorous as the sunset sign-off. Every day we deal with diarrhea, "scooting" (butt-sliding) dogs, arthritis, toenail trimming, and common surgeries. Over the past twenty-five years, I've done well over eight thousand ovariohysterectomies (spays), a well-practiced procedure now, but not exactly the stuff of sign-off music. We all get good at what we do frequently, no matter what our profession, but the *fun* stuff is the nonroutine.

Before I left the Air Force, our crew was chosen to fly our tanker low and fast over Riverfront Stadium in Cincinnati while the national anthem was played at the start of a Bengals game. A kid's dream realized!

The stories in this next group are examples of opportunity knocking only once. Included in the mix are a runaway goat, a midget owl, an ice-bound swan, some mysteriously multiplying skunks, and a two-legged cat. These cases are anything but routine; they are national-anthem flights of veterinary practice. Fasten your seat belts . . .

Escapegoat

Goats can make you crazy. I know this to be true because I've seen it happen. One minute a cattleman is sitting at the stockyard sale arena with the other farmers, waiting for his feeder calves to sell. His wife, who came along for the first time in years just to get away for the morning, sees a little Nubian kid with long, dangly ears and a noble Roman nose brought into the ring for sale. She leans over and says, "Oh look, honey, isn't it darling? Can't we take it home? It's going to sell for only ten dollars." Six months later, there are twenty-five of the beasts around in back of the barn and they've become a "goat dairy."

Goats are cute, and they're cheap, and if I had to describe their personality, I'd say that they are to ruminants (cud-chewers) what chimps are to primates. They're intelligent and they can find ways of getting into trouble that most farmers had never considered when they said, "OK, sweetie, but just this one."

Goats don't really eat cans like you see them do in cartoons. They eat the can-label paste. Then they chew the can. They lick the salt off the side of your car or truck in the winter, leaving a fish-scale pattern of tongue tracks in their wake. They love to climb. How will they know there isn't something good to eat on the roof of your car if they don't go up and look? They are smart, friendly, trainable, and gregarious. If you get one such terrific package for only ten bucks, the rest will follow. At least the farmer's wife comes along on sale day at the yard now.

One particular goat that had been sold at the stockyard became a popular subject for discussion one year. It hadn't rained for almost three weeks and the farmers were all complaining. A dry spell like this in the summer is great for weekend picnic planning, but terrible for crops. No rain, no growth of corn or soybeans. They'd been planted with considerable effort and expense and if the yield wasn't good, the farmers would lose not only their profits, but their investment in seed, weed-killer, fertilizer, and the diesel fuel to spread them. When a drought reaches a critical stage, farmers talk about nothing else. So a new topic for discussion in the coffee shop was a welcome relief.

It was hot and humid when Jack Ryan came into the office. "Doc, do you have a tranquilizer gun? I've got a problem with a goat."

"What kind of problem, Jack?"

"I've got a big billy goat that got loose from my farm and I can't catch him. He's been gone for almost a week now, and every time someone calls to tell me where he is, he moves before I get there."

"Where is he now?"

"He's up behind the library, near the high school. When I see him, I'd like to zap him with something so he'll go to sleep and we can load him in a trailer."

"Behind the library? Why did he come to town? I would think he'd head for the country instead of hanging out here."

"He cut across my back fields and down behind the Dairy Queen. He was seen hanging out there for a couple of days getting in the Dumpster. No one knew who owned him, and I was looking in the woods behind my barn while he was over there. He likes to eat flowers too, and he cleaned out the flower bed that was under the DQ sign. I'm afraid he'll be hit by a car or cause an accident, and I'm afraid I'll be liable if something bad happens."

"I don't have a tranquilizer gun, Jack."

"I thought every vet had a tranquilizer gun."

"That's just in the movies. Doc Hoggsett and Doc Williamson used to have them, but they'd deny it when someone asked them. When they died, the guns must have been sold. No one wants to be the one who's called when something happens that makes you need a tranquilizer gun. Remember when the bull got loose from the stock-yard and freight-trained the city treasurer in front of the courthouse? Remember when the sixteen-point buck crashed through the front window of the Church of Christ and ate the altar flowers? Or the time that crazy Akita of Jerry Lykan's ran into the Cut and Curl and terrorized the only partially-beautified patrons? Would you want to be the one they call to go chase down critters like these? The best reason not to have a tranquilizer gun is that 95 percent of the time, farmers would want me to use it to hunt down a wild heifer in the woods instead of herding her into the barn lot themselves before I got there. It would be a phenomenal timewaster in practice, and dangerous for cattle. Besides, I don't even know where to buy one."

"Gottcha, but what can I use to catch him? We can't herd him into a corner uptown."

"He's just a goat, Jack. Why don't you just grab him? He can't be too ferocious."

"He's not some old Nubian. This guy has horns like a Texas longhorn and weighs several hundred pounds. He's a huge exotic that I bought in a moment of weakness. Man, what a mistake."

"Bill Lukhart used to talk about using syringe-tipped arrows to tranquilize cattle that were wild. We could try that. Can you shoot a bow and hit something?"

"I used to bow hunt years ago and was pretty lousy at it, but I can try."

"Let's see if we can make the arrows first. Can you go down to Town and Country and get a few arrow shafts?"

"I have all morning off. I'll go down right now and be back in a flash."

He was back in half an hour. "Boy, it's hot out. That goat must be sleeping somewhere in the shade. Will these do?" He held up three nocked fiberglass arrow shafts.

"Let's see," I said, holding a 3-cc syringe near the end. "I think it's perfect. We'll remove the rubber tip from the syringe plunger and glue it on the end of the arrow shaft. The shaft will become the new plunger. We'll only need about .2 cc's of tranquilizer, so the arrow shaft can be inserted almost all the way into the barrel of the syringe. Instead of an arrowhead, the syringe's 18-gauge needle will stick in the goat. On impact, the arrow will move forward pushing the drug into the goat's rear end."

We made three tranquilizer arrows. A foolproof plan.

Two days later, Jack came into the office. "Doc, I need to reload the arrow syringes. So far, I've tranquilized two maple trees and the side of Harriet Wilson's house. She's enjoyed the goat's visits to her backyard, though. He's been spending the night in the woods next to her sun-porch, and she has her morning coffee watching him eat in her garden."

Harriet lived in a huge Tudor house next door to the library. She had donated some of her land for the library years ago and still had enough left to be fairly isolated in a woodland setting with a lot of ornamental plantings and flowers. The goat had good taste. He could eat imported shrubbery at Harriet's house, and give her a little enter-tainment in the process.

I reloaded the syringes and put on new needles to replace the bent ones that had missed their mark. "I don't need to tell you to be careful with these, do I, Jack?"

"I'll be careful," he reassured me.

A week passed and I hadn't seen Jack. I heard stories about the goat from a variety of interested people. He had spent a few nights on the front porch of Jimmy Wilburn, the country singer. Jimmy's Rolls Royce was parked near the porch and he really didn't want the Rolls to smell like a goat, or have its shiny flying lady chewed off by the horned fugi-tive. Flower beds all over town were being decimated by an unknown assailant. Footprints were seen on porches, drive-ways, and gliders, and an unusual musky odor accompanied the invasions. Most people didn't know who owned the goat and Jack preferred it that way. Who do you call when a huge goat with horns is on your porch? Not the dog warden. Usu-ally, people called the police. The police would call Jack.

Jack came to the office just before lunch. "Doc, we need a new plan. I can't hit a bull in the butt with a bass fiddle. I stuck an arrow eight feet up the side of Vance's garage. Any other suggestions?"

"Maybe. Tim Libre has those roping competitions out at his place for the kids. Why don't you call him and see if a couple of the guys that rope calves can rope the goat? Some of those guys can do pretty amazing things with a lariat. If they can rope the back feet of a running calf from the back of a horse, a goat shouldn't be a challenge."

"Good idea. I know him pretty well. I'll call him from my office."

Rain finally came in the form of a thunderstorm. Enough to help the crops and raise the humidity to near intolerable levels. The coffee shop talk changed from the weather to the goat of Jack Ryan. The secret was out. Everyone knew who owned the goat now. It had even been on the radio.

A new problem developed: The goat got wet in the storm, and nothing smells worse than a wet billy goat. It was bad enough when he was dry, but now he was a real stinker. This was a huge goat with an equally huge smell, now camping on a different front porch every night. The calls were coming to Jack's business office daily. Goat sightings. Smell reports.

Another week passed. Jack came into the office. "Doc, the guys are having trouble roping him because of those huge horns. What can we do next? They say they could rope him if they were on horseback, but not on foot and in town. They get near him and he runs through yards, over cars, between buildings, over fences. They're afraid they might be making the situation worse."

"Do you want to try to give him some grain with tranquilizers in it? We'll have to be careful with the dose. If we give him too much, it might hurt him."

"I'll try anything. The police are afraid he'll cause an accident, and they're talking about shooting him. Someone almost hit him with a Jeep last night when he crossed the street near Harriet's house."

I measured some powdered tranquilizer that I used for horses. "Put this in about a half pound of horse sweetfeed. He'll smell the feed from a hundred yards away. It should be enough to slow him down. Third time's the charm, right, Jack?"

Several days passed and Jack came into the office, smiling. "We got him!"

"Great! Did he eat the tranquilizer?" I asked.

"Nope, he wouldn't come near it. But it got me thinking about something else. When you said that he would come from a hundred yards away for the food, maybe he would come for a female in heat. We tied a nanny in heat in the front of a cattle trailer, and parked it up near the library, where we saw him last. We left the back door open. Within an hour he was near the trailer and went inside to investigate. Wham! We slammed the back door shut and he was ours. I drove him directly to the stockyard, and he'll go in the ring tomorrow on sale day. I don't care what he brings, but while we were unloading him, a guy and his wife were watching. She said, 'Oh look, honey. Isn't that big goat darling? Do you think we could buy him? I just love him!'"

"OK, sweetie, but just this one."

Slow but Steady

When you live near a lake, you must have a boat. I had a good small boat that the family enjoyed. If we had so much fun with a boat this size, a bigger boat would surely be even more fun. I traded my good boat for seven thousand pounds of future firewood on a trailer—a 27-year-old riverboat with more dry rot topside than mahogany. But I loved it, and spent most of the summer of 1987 repairing its soft spots and filling them with Bondo fiberglass auto-body filler. It was a 26-foot Owens cruiser named Speedwell, but it could just as easily have been named Bondo. After a new paint job it would be the prettiest boat on the lake. Who needs a fiberglass boat when you can have real wood? Mostly wood, anyway. The Speedwell was kept on a trailer behind my office and I worked on it there on the weekends. I was finishing some last-minute touch-ups on the brightwork when Mrs. Murphy came alongside in her car.

"Dr. Sharp, are you up there?" she asked.

I looked down from the deck and saw her gray hair sticking out of the car window. Mrs. Florence Murphy was a widow, and a perfect lady. She was in her seventies, plump, well-coiffed, proper, and dignified, and she was wearing sensible shoes and a blue dress with white polka dots.

"Hi, Mrs. Murphy. How's Jody?" Jody was an overweight, ten-year-old terrier who frequently had problems with her "scooter."

"She's fine, and of course sends her love. I was pulling out of my driveway and found this poor turtle in the road. Can you see if you can help him?"

I stepped over the taffrail, and onto the top of the aluminum stepladder that I used to climb aboard. The top of the Speedwell's cabin was thirteen feet above the ground. Holding on to the boat made the trip down the ladder less shaky. "Let's see what he looks like."

"I'm afraid a car ran over him and broke his shell," said Mrs. Murphy.

In the cardboard box she held out to me was a large male box turtle. His shell had cracks radiating out from a hole in the center. The missing circular area was about three inches in diameter, and exposed the naked turtle underneath. He was, of course, tucked in tightly. I could see his eyes and he appeared alert, but having an injury to his shell that was this extensive, he probably had internal injuries as well.

Not everyone would swerve out of the way of a box turtle crossing the road. Too bad. But Mrs. Murphy thought enough of him to pick him up and drive to town to get help for him. She was upset and worried that he might die. How could I possibly tell her that I knew nothing about turtles? Especially squashed turtles. "He really does have a bad crack in his shell. Maybe we could wire the cracks so that they might heal, but I'm not sure what to do about that big hole."

"I'll leave him with you, Dr. Sharp. I know that you'll take good care of him."

Good care of him? I was clueless. I went to the bait shop at the edge of town and got some wax worms. Do turtles eat wax worms? This one did. I used a drill with a small bit and drilled holes that would allow stainless steel orthopedic wire to pull the radiating cracks together. He had a more solid shell now, but what could I use to cover the hole?

I put the turtle in his box, gave him some more wax worms, and went back up the ladder to finish varnishing the Speedwell. All of a sudden it occurred to me that I had a great deal of experience with this type of problem. I was the Bondo King of West Main Street. I jumped to the ladder, went down in a hurry, and ran into the office. I smeared Vaseline on the naked part of the turtle that was exposed by the shell defect (I didn't want the body putty to stick to the tissue under the shell), then I mixed up the fiberglass body-putty and filled 'er in! Just like another hole in the Speedwell. I even drew a pattern in the brown putty to make it match the other parts of the shell. It hardened like a rock.

If Mrs. Murphy was going to have to bury her turtle, he was at least going to go out looking good. I really thought his chances were poor at best. He had, after all, been squashed.

The next day was routine until Mrs. Murphy came to the office. "Oh Dr. Sharp, I've been up worrying about the turtle most of the night."

"You know, he was really badly injured," I said. "Why don't you take him back home and let him go near the woods." I thought that if he wandered into the woods to die, this way she wouldn't have to know.

"He looks so good! I'm going to feed him by hand until he gets his strength back."

I guessed she *was* going to be there when he died. Too bad.

Two weeks went by and Mrs. Murphy phoned. "Dr. Sharp, I wanted you to know, I just let our turtle go free. He crawled off into the woods and was doing very well. Thanks again." I told the office staff and we were all amazed, not only at Mrs. Murphy's dedication, but at the tough little guy in the Bondo shell.

Two years passed, and each took its toll on the Speedwell. No matter what I used to cover her in the fall, I had to scrape and paint her every spring. The trailer rusted and had to be painted. The varnish peeled and needed to be reapplied. The dry rot progressed like a cancer. I was learning why people buy fiberglass boats.

In May, chubby Jody Murphy was in the office to have her frequent scooting problem fixed, and Mrs. Murphy was excited. "Dr. Sharp, I saw our turtle! He was about a mile from home crossing the road near the Belfast store. I know it was our turtle because his shell had that funny brown stuff that you used on it!"

"Really! When did you see him?"

"Last week."

My heart sank. I had hoped that she had just seen him, and that we could find him again and take a picture for a quirky journal article. "Did you stop and say hello for us?"

"I did better than that. I picked him up and drove him home. I let him go free out in our woods where he belongs."

"If you should see him again, will you call me?"

"Of course," said Jody's favorite human.

Six more years ticked off, and in 1995, the roof on the office was starting to show some wear. It was time for new shingles. The Speedwell had not been put in the water for two years and was looking every bit its age, thirty-five years old now, and peeling like an abandoned house. One of the roofers wanted to buy it and restore it, and I thought it sounded like a great idea. The size of his offer was definitely no object. She was outta there in less time than it took to say dry rot.

One evening in August, I saw Mrs. Murphy pull into the office parking lot. She came in carrying a cardboard box. *He was back!* The turtle's patch was eight years old now, and faded to a light tan color, but it was as tight as the day the Bondo had been smeared into his wound. The stainless steel wire was no longer visible. "I found him in the road again, this time near the Fairfax store, about two miles cross-country from home!" Pictures were taken and we all laughed in disbelief. "I'm going to put him back in his woods where he belongs."

His patch lasted longer than the patches in the Speedwell. I haven't seen him again since that day, but I never pass a turtle on the road that I don't slow down and look at its shell. Turtles live a long time. Please be careful.

Night Flyer

John Davis is our local game warden. He works for the State of Ohio and is actually called a game protector. Sure, he carries a gun, arrests poachers, wears a uniform, and might ask to see your fishing license, but he is an animal lover at heart, which is why he has this job. Over the years, when people would call him about injured animals and he thought they could be fixed, he would bring them to the office for an opinion, and sometimes treatment. On or off duty, he carried a large metal mailbox in his truck that would hold small game, or birds as large as great horned owls or red-tailed hawks. When John came into the office carrying his mailbox, a surprise was always in store.

I particularly enjoyed the hawks he brought in. Hawks sometimes crash into wires, buildings, cars, or other solid objects while concentrating on prey. John would bring them in for radiographs to see if a wing fracture was present or repairable. Sometimes they were just knocked senseless, and a few days at the bird infirmary was all they needed. It's hard to hunt with a headache.

It's easy to see why hawks are so trainable. They're suckers for chicken, and if you're patient, they'll soon get over their fear of people. On its first day in captivity, a hawk might not eat, but during the night, the chicken pieces would disappear. On the second day, it might eat, but only in the back of the cage with its wings out-stretched to hide what it was doing. On the third day, it would be waiting at the cage door, and would take the morsel from my hand. Some hawks don't discriminate between chicken parts and finger parts, so gloves are always in order, but examining a big bird is really pretty easy. I have a pair of leather welding gloves that protect my hands from their sharp talons, so it's not hard to reach into the cage and grab both legs with one hand. I can support the bird and examine the rest of it with an ungloved free hand. For some reason, big birds rarely bite, so if you control their feet, the rest is easy.

Great horned owls are a little harder to handle. The quiet, dignified-looking, wise old owl sitting on the branch is really the most feared predator of the night woods. The talons on a great horned owl are like two-inch hooked ice picks, and if one of these big guys grabs your arm, it's hard to get it to let go, since they grip like a vise. I usually only handle great horned owls with someone else present. If no one is around, a pair of vise grips in my back pocket makes me feel safer because I could use them to pry the talons out of my forearm. With a wingspread of up to five feet, it's easy to see how a great horned owl could swoop down and grab a small animal. They are silent, flying, night stalkers.

It was October, and we were putting up Halloween decorations in the office when John and his mailbox came in the front door.

"Hi, John. What's in the box?" I asked.

"You'll like this one, Doc. He's just a little guy."

He put the mailbox on the front counter and I asked, "Can I open it?"

"Be my guest."

"Bird or mammal?" I at least wanted to know if it would run out at me or fly out.

"Take a look."

I slowly lowered the door and peeked in at the littlest owl I had ever seen. It was gray, and had tufted ears like a great horned owl, but instead of being two feet high, this little guy was only about seven inches tall. One eye was closed and the other looked in at its nose. It obviously had a head injury.

"Is this a screech owl, John? I've never seen one up close."

"Good guess, Doc. He must have flown into a car or something. Mabel Odiel found him walking down the side of the road out by her place on Pigeon Roost Road. She picked him up and put him under a peach basket until I could go get him. I think he has a little blood coming out of his ear. His eyes are the big problem."

I reached into the mailbox, grabbed the owl around his middle so that his wings were held against his body, and brought him out for a good look. "What a cute little guy. Is this all the bigger he'll get?"

"Yup. That's it. He's an adult."

"What do these little owls eat, John? I keep chicken in the freezer in case we have a hawk, but he probably wouldn't like that, would he?"

"They eat big insects in the wild. They also eat mice and little birds. He is a predator but on a smaller scale than the big owls. He might like chicken."

"Since he can't see anyway, maybe he'll eat whatever we put in his mouth. I'll go down to Schelling's bait shop at noon and find something for him. One thing is certain. He can't find his own food if he can't see. I'll give him a cortisone shot and feed him for a while. Let's see if he can get better with a little TLC."

"Thanks, Doc. Call me if you need something, and let me know how he makes out."

We soon discovered that if we placed a wax worm in the owl's mouth, he ate it. He ate like a starving teenage football player. He was never fussy. If we gave it to him, he'd eat it. Small pieces of chicken were a favorite with him. Each day I gave him an injection of an anti-inflammatory drug in the breast muscles. We used an insulin syringe with a fine needle, and he never flinched. After a week, his closed eye stayed open; his apparent headache was subsiding, but his pupils were not the same size. This is pretty easy to determine when eyes are as big as an owl's. He'd had a concussion and was not able to focus his eyes yet, so he had no depth perception and couldn't hunt effectively.

By the second week, he started to enjoy his vacation. He would take food from anyone's bare fingers, and liked to ride around on your shoulder like a pirate's parrot. His needle-like little talons would cling to clothing like Velcro. He was very affectionate and would walk up and down our hands enjoying an occasional rub behind the ears. He weighed next to nothing, and felt like a fluff of feathers with a few bones underneath.

If we were going to release him, he'd have to start flying and hunting for his food. We practiced enticing him with a morsel and throwing it to the ground. He would launch from my shoulder and land near the food, but he couldn't find it. At least he didn't crash into the ground, and he seemed to have some depth perception returning.

Gradually, he started to enjoy playing "fly to the food." After one more week his pupils were finally the same size, and we decided it was time to let him try this outside. Time to release our new friend.

We all went outside to watch the big launch. I held him in the air and gently pitched him skyward. Unexpectedly, he fluttered to the ground and sat there, as if to say: Where's the food?

"What do you think's the matter?" Melissa asked.

"Beats me. I know he can see, and I know he can fly, so I'm not sure what's wrong now."

Susie said, with the common sense that the rest of us seemed to have left at home that day, "Isn't he nocturnal?"

"Oops. I'll bet you're right. Let's take him inside and do this tonight before we close up for the night."

After work, at about 6:30 on the October evening that is called "Beggar's Night" in Hillsboro, we tried another launch. This time he flew off into the woods behind the office.

The little screech owl must have liked his new environment, because for a long time after that we could hear his hollow whistles and eery trembling calls. Superstitious people, when they hear this spooky cry, think that bad luck—or even death—must be near. We know it's just our little pal, happy to be home, and just in time for Halloween.

The Rescue

It had been snowing for four days. School had been called off because the busses couldn't negotiate the hills and curves of the Highland County back roads. Just when we thought it was over and a warming trend was in the cards, the rain started, and a layer of ice covered the deep snow. The trees were beautiful with their icy coating, and the cedars were bending over from the weight of their new burden. Of course driving was difficult, and most of our scheduled appointments had canceled, but we were open for emergencies.

"Dr. Sharp, Mary Neil is on the phone and says she has an emergency," Melissa said.

"What kind of emergency?" I asked, knowing that the Highland County humane officer could serve up just about anything. Abuse cases, abandoned horses, parrots suffering from smoke inhalation, and many more.

"I don't know. She didn't say."

I picked up the phone and took it off hold. "Hi, Mary! How are you?"

"Fine, Rob, but we have a weird problem that I hope you can help us with. We have a swan down on the ice and his feet are frozen to it. He can't move and we're afraid he'll die there. He's out in the middle of an eighty-acre field and has been there overnight. Dave Freel saw him there yesterday evening and he was still there this morning when Dave went to work."

"Has anyone tried to go out to him?" I asked.

"Nope. I just learned of it. We know that he'll need to be treated for frostbite so I called you first."

"Mary, I've never been up close to a swan. How do you handle one?"

"It's only a bird. Think of it as a big duck."

"I was thinking of it more as a big goose, and I've run from them more than once. I've been attacked by both geese and barnyard turkeys."

"Truthfully, I've never been near one either. Better be a little careful. They probably have pretty good pecking range with a neck that long."

I put on my insulated coveralls, coat, boots, scarf, and ball cap and prepared to go out on a "swan call." The field that "held" the swan was only a mile from the office but it took about twenty minutes to get there due to the ice.

There it was. Sitting in the exact middle of the field. The eighty-acre field. It was a white bump in a sea of white. Only its bill was a contrasting color. Whatever I was going to need for this project would have to be carried all the way from the truck to the bird, so a little forethought was needed. I selected my drug bag, some udder cream for its feet, a small lariat for possible restraint (what did I know about swan restraint?), and a broom for self-defense. I started across the field, slogging through the deep snow with the icy frosting. Dr. Zhivago.

As I approached the swan I started to notice how big it was. This was no duck. I was a city boy who'd read *The Ugly Duckling* as a kid. No one would mistake a Cessna-like duck for this B-52. The swan's head rose as I approached. What a neck! And then it stood up. Its head must have been above my waist. How did I let Mary talk me into this? This bird might be stuck to the ice, but that beak wasn't stuck to anything! How could I examine its feet and avoid that big beak at the same time?

"Whoa, boy," was the best I could come up with. The swan replied with some kind of noise that I couldn't interpret. Probably just as well. I was eight feet away when I thought of the rope. If I could get the rope around that huge neck, I might control the bird a little. I put down the bag and the broom and prepared for my cowboy lasso act. I coiled up the lariat, made an open loop in my right hand, and let her fly.

I missed. Damn. I tried again, and hit the swan in the snoot. That was apparently the last time it was going to let me try. It lowered its head, stretched out its neck, and started to make that noise again—this time with its wings outstretched and flapping. It looked like it was mad, and it was coming right toward me! "Hey, you're stuck to the ice!" I said, dropping the lariat in favor of the broom. The swan covered that eight feet between us before I got out the word "hey." Now it was biting me on the arm and whacking me with its huge wings. Before I could grab the broom, the bird was airborne. It circled the field to get its compass reset, and flew off over the ice-covered woods.

Helpless, gentle creature. Stuck to the ice. Right. Maybe it was just taking a siesta.

After my hands quit shaking, I picked up my stuff, followed my own tracks back to the truck, and wondered how I could waste the rest of the day.

"I have good news, Mary. The swan is on its way and its feet are OK," was the report given.

Next time she was coming with me.

The Class of 1990

Ask any old physician, and he or she will tell you that the best way to really know your patients is to visit them at home. House calls give you a true picture of a person.

Ask any old veterinarian, and he or she will tell you that you get to know your patients when you board them. When you feed, walk, play with, and clean up after them for a week or two, you see a side of the animal that no yearly examination will ever demonstrate.

Ask any old teacher to tell you about the most memorable kids in his or her classes, and you'll hear about the very nice, and the very bad ones. The average ones fade in our memory, but the exceptional stand out. So it is with the Class of 1990.

Six dogs were contemporaries, and all of them spent time boarding with us over a decade or so. We knew them all very well and they, too, fell into the teachers' categories—the very good and the very bad.

Trix Burke was a happy little wiener dog who, when he was rejoicing, could shoot a stream of urine two feet in the air. When it became necessary to pick him up, you had to point him in a safe direction until his first squirt of gladness had passed. You never, ever, let him roll on his back.

I met Trix on the day that I bought the practice from Dr. Lukhart, in July of 1980. Mrs. Burke was a tiny lady in her seventies who had made arrangements to board him with Dr. Lukhart, not Dr. Sharp, and was very upset when she arrived. After all, she didn't even know me and she was leaving Trix, her only companion, with a total stranger for two weeks. After a brief introduction, she decided that I would have to do. It was too late to make other arrangements.

She placed the palm of her hand against Trix's lips and kissed the back of her hand. No germs, you know. She handed him to me and I experienced the first "Trix Salute."

While Mrs. Burke was doing floor exercises at the health spa in California, she suffered a heart attack. By the time she was well enough to travel again, Trix had spent over six months with us. When Mrs. Burke returned, I took Trix out to greet her. He ran up to her, urinated on her shoes, and ran back to jump up in my arms. "I guess he got along OK," she said.

With the exception of his one problem, which you quickly learned to deal with, Trix was a wonderful little guy with a tail that always whipped back and forth to signal his approval.

Gyp McNeil was a twenty-pound mutt, and very vocal. His real name was Gypsy, but because of all the money he'd cost his foster owners over the years, they felt that Gyp was more appropriate. They called themselves "foster" owners since his real owner, their neighbor, had died of cancer, and when no one wanted Gyp, they had taken him in. Only temporarily. They said that they didn't want him permanently. They didn't even like dogs. They'd had him for fourteen years.

Gyp was the only dog we have ever boarded who could talk. He must have enjoyed it too, because he did it all the time. He said "OW!" as if he were hurt. OW! OW! OW! OW! During the ten years that I knew him, he spent the summers with us while his foster owners spent summers in Arizona. For four months of every year, I heard Gyp in the kennel, pretending to be hurt. OW!

Shorty Green was the perfect dog. He never did anything

wrong. He was a shepherd-collie cross who was named Shorty because he was expected to be a small dog. Had he been given the training, he could easily have been an assistance dog. He could learn to do anything in a very short time.

Shorty stayed with us so often that his owner had a key to the office so she could leave him or get him after hours. He had his favorite cage and his favorite outside run, and he knew the office routine like an employee. His owner would occasionally stick him in the front door, and he would run back to the kennel and wait by his favorite cage. He loved people, was friendly with other dogs, never barked, never thought of biting, and was never sick. What more could you ask for?

It was a rare day when one of these three dogs was not with us.

The other three members of the class, Bobby Jaimeson, O. J. Brooks, and Angel Nash had two things in common: They loved their owners, and they hated everyone else. While they stayed with us, they were not above biting the hand that was feeding them.

Bobby bit me as a six-week-old puppy, and then got meaner as he got older. He was tricky to feed because of a congenital enlargement of his esophagus. If his food was not placed up on a chair, it would not drop into his stomach when he swallowed. It would collect in a pouch that formed between his mouth and his stomach and then he would vomit. So every meal was fed to him on a chair, with extreme caution by the feeder to avoid being the appetizer. He was very predictable and always nasty.

Angel Nash was a fat mixed-breed attitude case. He always suffered from anal sac impactions and could scoot, nonstop, across a hundred-yard football field. We frequently had to try to treat his south end without having an unpleasant encounter with his north.

O. J. Brooks was a Lhasa apso that must have thought he was guarding the royal palace in Tibet. He had a face like a thunderstorm and would bite anything in range.

These three were frequent boarders too, but, luckily, not often in the office simultaneously. They each required special handling and each took additional time to feed, clean, and even move from place to place. After ten years of boarding, they never warmed up to us. They were always in a bad mood. They were never to be trusted.

One weekend in the summer of 1990, all six dogs were in the office at the same time. They were all very old now, and it was obvious. Shorty would wait by his cage with his legs trembling from spinal arthritis. Trix, the fountain, had a snow-white face and cataracts in both eyes. Gyp could barely walk, and only said OW! if you touched him.

The bad three were all there as well, but not to be boarded. Bobby had pneumonia for about the tenth time, from aspirating food due to his megaesophagus. Angel was diabetic, and having trouble with renal failure. O. J. had a bladder stone.

I looked around at my pals in the kennel and felt like we had become the nursing home for old dogs. For the first time in their lifetimes, the "bad three" let me pet them. Bobby rolled his lips back, but never moved. O. J. actually seemed to enjoy a little affection, and Angel was too sick to object.

I knew these six would never be back together again, and I would have liked them to pose for a group photo. I felt bad that they were aging, and wouldn't be with us much longer.

All six died within the year. I felt as if I were a part owner of all of them, and when I was asked to euthanize Shorty, I didn't know if I could do it. Maybe another veterinarian. But it is, after all, something to be done by a friend. Making him less miserable was the last thing that I could do for him. It still wasn't easy.

One by one, the Class of 1990 left us. It was also the year that we stopped boarding. A new boarding kennel opened in town, and I needed our kennel space for hospitalized dogs and cats.

The last to go was Gyp McNeil. He was sixteen years old and dying of renal failure. He could no longer eat due to ulcers in his intestines. As I inserted the catheter into his leg and attached the syringe full of euthanasia solution, I looked up at his crying "foster" owner.

"He's not even my dog," the old man said.

I bit my lip and gave the dog the solution. Gyp laid his head on the blanket, and for the last time, softly, said "ow."

The Beast in the Basement

Some people don't deserve a dog, or any other animal. They probably don't deserve a spouse, kids, or friends either. The difference is that the spouse, kids, and friends can leave, but the dog is stuck with the jerk. Compared to the abuse some animals suffer at the hands of undeserving humans, abandonment might be preferable. In extreme cases, the courts get involved and the animal is rescued. So it was in the summer of 1991 when I met the beast in the basement.

"Holy cats!" I jumped up as the three-in-the-morning phone call startled me. "Hello."

"Dr. Sharp, this is Captain Davis of the Hillsboro Police Department. We have a situation and we need some advice."

"What kind of situation?"

"We have a suspect, a known drug user, who is drunk out of his mind, and he's been attacked by a dog. We think it's his own dog. We're going to have to take the suspect to the hospital and we don't know what to do with the dog."

"Where's the dog?"

"He's down in the basement growling. He's a big chow and there aren't any lights down there. The officer can see him with his flashlight, but he says that all he can see are teeth and green eyes. There's a lot of dog poop down there and it looks like he probably lives there. Do you think we should shoot him or do you want to come over and catch him?"

"Neither. Don't shoot him. He just bit someone and the health department needs to make sure he's rabies free. If you shoot him in the head, he can't be tested. If you shoot him somewhere else he might bite the shooter. There's no real reason to shoot him. We just need to quarantine him. Is the house secure?"

"We'll lock it up when we leave."

"Make sure that he has food and water and just lock him in the house until morning. I'll talk to the humane officer and dog warden then."

"Thanks, Doc. Sorry to call you so late."

The next morning I called Mary Neil, the humane officer, and told her the story. She said she'd find out the address and make arrangements to get the dog.

At noon, a man with his arm in a sling came bursting into the office with a big red chow on a chain. The man was loud, twitchy, dirty, and obviously under the influence of something. The dog gave the ominous "chow stare" they can all do so well.

"May I help you?" Melissa asked the disheveled walk-in.

"My dog's been hurt and I want the vet to fix him."

"What's wrong with him?"

"Me and him got into a little altercation over a pizza that I brought home from the Sail Inn and I accidentally stabbed him. The knife blade broke off in him somewhere."

So this was the guy. Out of the hospital.

"What happened to your arm?" I asked.

"The son of a bitch bit me. I have fifteen or twenty tooth marks. I was hurt real bad. The hospital just released me and I have to be in court in half an hour."

"I'll take care of him. Just hand me his leash. What's his name?"

"'Beast'—and whatever you do, don't let him get a whiff of alcohol. He gets real mean if he smells it," advised the authority on alcohol.

I walked back to the treatment area with Beast on a leash, being a little careful of the dog that put the jerk in the hospital. He had the potential of doing the same to me. Where was the stab wound?

Beast was limping slightly on his left front leg. He seemed to breathe without difficulty and didn't seem to be bleeding anywhere.

I squatted down on the floor to get a better look at the assailant, reached over slowly, and patted him on the head. His stare was penetrating and his eyes never left mine. Then his tail wagged. His stare continued, but there was a chink in the tough guy's armor. I looked at the floor and continued to pet his head and ears. I didn't want him to feel threatened by too much eye contact. He took a step toward me and licked my ear. It may have been the first time in his life that someone was nice to him.

We needed to find his wound, so I sat on the floor and continued to pet him, paying particular attention to the hair over the areas that I palpated, looking for dried blood or other evidence of a stab wound. I wasn't completely trusting since I knew he would defend himself if he thought it was necessary. I moved slowly, and we both kept an eye on each other. X-rays would probably be needed. He smelled terrible and was matted and filthy.

"Melissa, can you get the 14x17 x-ray cassettes ready? Let's give him a tranquilizer and take a look at his front half."

Carefully, I administered a subcutaneous injection of a tranquilizer, and gradually, the Beast became a lamb. We took a lateral view of his front half and the same view of the rear just to scout around. The jerk said he'd broken the knife in the process of stabbing the dog. Maybe we could see the wound.

Ten minutes later, the x-rays were out of the developer and Melissa said, "You won't believe what you're going to see."

I held the dripping film up to the view box and there, along the outside surface of the humerus of his upper left leg, was the five-inch blade of a steak knife. I anesthetized Beast.

Melissa clipped the hair from the dog's leg and prepared it for surgery while I called the humane officer. I wanted her to know the details so that Beast would not be returned to the dog-stabbing jerk.

We found the entry wound and dissected down until metal was visible. What kind of a person stabs a dog that tries to eat his pizza?

I was somehow glad the Beast had gotten his licks in.

The jerk knew he'd made a mistake when the eighty-four-pound dog was dangling from his arm.

I pulled out the blade and sutured the wound. As Beast was waking up, Melissa and I took turns talking to him and patting his head. His tail wagged every time. This was not a vicious dog. This dog was just not going to take it anymore, and he was of a breed to do something about it.

After the anesthetic wore off, we put him in a cage and kept him for over a week. During this time he behaved like a normal dog. We gave him antibiotic capsules three times a day by just sticking them in his lips.

Beast was never aggressive, and enjoyed his walks outside. By the end of the week, I called Mary Neil.

"What are we going to do with our attack dog, Mary? His quarantine for rabies is going to be up soon and he'll need a home. Will the judge allow us to give him away before the cruelty hearing?"

"I already have a foster home, and if the judge says it's OK, they'll keep him for good."

"Sounds great. Let me know and I'll take him out to the shelter."

I vaccinated Beast and delivered him into Mary's care.

About a year later a young couple came into the office to get their dog's annual exam and vaccinations. They were the Jacobys and their chow was named Willie. I examined him from head to tail, while he wiggled and licked me.

"How old is Willie?" I asked.

"We really don't know. We got him at the animal shelter. They said he'd been abused, and was taken away from his previous home by the court. They said he'd even been stabbed. Your name is on his shot record."

"Stabbed?"

I never would have guessed that the big red fluffy chow I had just examined was the dog who had stayed with us for almost two weeks. While I hadn't recognized him, he may have remembered us. He was cheerful, friendly, and even enjoyed being examined. I looked at Willie's happy face, and knew that the Beast was gone.

Taxi

Harriet always came to the office in a taxi. At that time, Hillsboro had only one taxi, and the same person had been driving it for years. If you needed to go to an appointment, Doris would pick you up and take you there. Of course you wouldn't be the only person in the cab since other people had to go places too. If Doris was downtown, picking up someone at the coffee shop, and heading out to the new shopping area, there might be five of you in the car together. This wasn't all bad, because you were likely to know most of the people riding with you, and you could catch up on local news during the trip.

If someone needed to stop at the grocery store for only a few things, all of the passengers would wait in the cab while shopping proceeded. No sense coming back. By the end of your trip, you might have made a new friend, and renewed old acquaintances.

Proximity was everything. The closest passengers were picked up first, and the closest destination was the first stop. A direct trip was rare and you were expected to wait your turn. You could take a nice ride with Doris and fill an otherwise boring afternoon if you planned your stops correctly. Senior citizens especially enjoyed the service.

I'm not sure that Harriet enjoyed the service, though. Harriet was a cat, and most cats don't like a nice ride in a car. Her owner, Mrs. Willis Peters, was very old and didn't drive. She lived with Harriet and got along without much help, but she did need Doris and the taxi from time to time. Harriet was black, thin, and in cat years was at least as old as Mrs. Peters. The age of some females is a taboo subject, but I would guess that Harriet and Mrs. Peters were 17 and 90, respectively. They were friends and kept one another company. Old cats don't need much. A little food, water, and a warm place to sleep.

They lived together in a postage-stamp-size house, and even though Harriet went outside for daily necessities, she was never more than a few feet from the front door. One day she was "just not right," and Mrs. Peters phoned me.

"Why do you think Harriet is sick?" I asked.

"She seems very swollen, and she didn't eat a bite this morning. This is the first time in her life that she's missed a meal. I'm really worried, Dr. Sharp."

I looked down at the appointment book on the front desk. "I see that three o'clock is open today. Would that be convenient?"

"Doris isn't always on time, but I'll try to have Harriet there at three."

Doris isn't always on time. No kidding. I'm sure that she'll exercise her usual precision. Give or take an hour or so and the length of a shopping list. I wrote Mrs. Peters in the margin of the appointment book between 2:30 and 4:00 PM.

To our amazement, at precisely three o'clock, the big white Chevy Impala with TAXI on the side pulled into the parking lot. The bun on Doris's head was visible over the top of the steering wheel as we looked out of the front window of the office. On the back ledge of the cab was Harriet. No other passengers.

Doris carried Harriet to the front desk and said, "Hi, Doc. I guess you know what to do with this kitty. Maude said you could call her when you're through with her. See ya." She plunked Harriet on the counter, and out she went.

As I carried Harriet to the exam room I already agreed with Mrs. Peters. Her abdomen felt very swollen. I put her on the exam table and began to palpate her swollen stomach. I had spayed her many years before, so I knew she wasn't pregnant. The mass in her abdomen was huge and as hard as a summer sausage.

"Melissa, do you have time to take some radiographs of her abdomen?" I was falling behind on the afternoon schedule and Melissa could take the films and develop them without my help.

"Do you want films of just the abdomen or the whole body?"

"Maybe we ought to use the 14x17 plates and look at her whole body."

I saw the next few appointments, and then stopped to look at the developed films still dripping in the darkroom. I held the lateral view up to the light box, and the problem was obvious.

"Harriet has a megacolon," I said to Melissa. "What a whopper! She must have a week's worth of stool in there. The diameter of the colon is probably four times its normal size. Since she goes outside and doesn't use a litter pan, I'll bet Mrs. Peters never suspected that Harriet couldn't have a bowel movement."

"What are we gonna do?" Melissa asked.

"Well, as much as I hate to do it, we need to anesthetize her and give her multiple enemas until all this stool is out."

A megacolon is a mysterious problem. Sometimes it can be genetic, sometimes it's acquired late in life. The muscular, moving tube that normally propels digested food out of the body becomes flaccid, dilated, and almost useless, except as a holding place for stool. If we were able to relieve her obstipation, she would need medication and aftercare, or she would be right back here with the same problem.

We got out the "enema rig" as it has come to be known, and filled it with warm water to which I added the slipperiest stuff known to man—powdered glove lubricant used on the shoulder-length palpation sleeves of farm vets. A little powder, a little water, and instant slime. This would help Harriet pass the troublesome hardened mass of stool.

The details from here on are not necessary, but are exactly what you would expect. Suffice it to say that we were successful. Harriet was too sleepy to go home that night.

I called Mrs. Peters and told her of the problem. "Harriet will be fine, but she will have to be watched carefully so that this doesn't happen again. I'll send home a list of instructions. Because of her age, we don't want to give her another anesthetic if we can avoid it."

"I understand, Dr. Sharp. I want to do all I can for her."

"Some dietary changes will be necessary too."

"I'll feed her whatever you suggest."

The next day, Harriet was feeling much lighter and could go home. Rather than have Doris and the taxi pick her up, I just delivered her myself. She lived only a few blocks from the office. I didn't think Harriet would enjoy a possibly long ride home in the taxi, and I was going right by Mrs. Peters's house at lunchtime anyway. They were happy to see each other.

Two weeks later we had the instant replay. Same cab, same problem, same enema rig, same hassle, same result. I took Harriet home the next day. We discussed prevention again, this time in greater detail.

A month later we had another episode of obstipation. "This has got to stop," I said to Melissa. "It's no fun for any of us—especially Harriet."

This time there was a complication. When the cab pulled in it was five o'clock on a Saturday evening. I didn't want to give Harriet an anesthetic and go through this lengthy process this late in the day. Harriet would sleep for quite a while and I didn't want to watch a cat sleep until midnight, nor did I want to leave a seventeen-year-old cat anesthetized and unattended. We needed a new approach.

"Harriet, how would you like some hairball medicine?" I said, approaching her with a tube of malt-flavored petroleum jelly. The theory here was that if this stuff is used to go in one end of the gastrointestinal tract and slide, undigested, to the other end, lubricating hair and all to pass, then maybe it would help slide the problem stool along too, until tomorrow when we could replay the old tune.

Normally, when we only have a problem with hairballs, we recommend a teaspoon of this stuff twice a week. I squeezed, Harriet licked. I squeezed more, Harriet licked more. She really liked this stuff! This is an inert lubricant and can't hurt anything, even in large quantities. Keep squeezing, I told myself. She finished the entire tube and wanted more. What a cat. A cooperator. What a rarity.

I came in on Sunday morning expecting to get out the "enema rig," and walked in to greet Harriet. There, in her litter box, was a miracle. She had passed the contents of her megacolon, and had done it by herself. We had a new way to deal with this problem, and Harriet was a willing partner. I called Mrs. Peters and told her the good news. "Harriet will be fine if we give her a tablespoon or more of hairball medicine on top of her food every day."

I saw Harriet for a few more years, but only for vaccinations and minor problems. Her megacolon was under control and she lived the rest of her life in comfort.

I never saw Mrs. Peters again after the last time I took Harriet home. She always sent Harriet by herself in the taxi, with Doris as her chauffeur. Sometimes other people in the taxi had to wait while I examined and vaccinated the cat. They were very understanding. They knew that this time, it was Harriet's turn.

Who You Gonna Call?

One evening, close to sunset, I went out to take a little motorcycle ride. As I opened the garage door, I heard the sound of running feet and wondered what had been frightened by the opening door. It was dark in the garage, so I grabbed a flashlight off the shelf and looked under the truck. A pair of glowing eyes looked back at me. Probably a cat, I thought, but it was dark-colored and I needed to get closer to see it. I walked around to the other side of the truck, got down on my hands and knees, and held the flashlight on the critter. Trouble. I had just gone nose to nose with a skunk.

I turned off the light and backed up quickly. No sense frightening it anymore. I might already have passed the "discharge threshold." I went outside to think for a minute. What was I going to do with a skunk in there? I couldn't scare it out, and I couldn't move the truck. Starting the truck motor was out of the question. I've had experience with dogs that have been blasted by a skunk, and I know they can smell for more than a week. One false move and the garage would stink for a long time. This was an emergency. If I raised all the doors, maybe it would leave on its own. I slowly and quietly lifted the doors and watched.

The skunk waddled out as I had hoped. No residual odor. How had it gotten in? If it got in once, it might be back. I thought about that skunk every time I went into the garage, and so for the next few nights, I looked under my truck with a flashlight. On the third night, eyeballs looked back. It had returned, and apparently liked it in the garage. A new plan was needed.

I borrowed a live trap from Bill Lukhart, and set it near the edge of the garage. The skunk could enter either end of the cage and be caught if it stepped on the treadle in the middle. I used bologna as bait. It was flat and would stick to the treadle, and it was quite fragrant as well. I hoped that no skunk could resist bologna, although I didn't know if it was even something a skunk would eat. I just went under the assumption that all God's creatures should like bologna.

As I had hoped, it didn't resist the temptation. When I went out to the garage to go to work the next day, it was in the trap. Now a new problem arose. What do you do with a trapped skunk?

This could be really tricky. Why didn't I think of this before the skunk was in the cage? I went back in the house to tell Susie of my success as a trapper, hoping she might have a suggestion about the next step.

"Hey, Susie, guess what I caught last night?"

"Don't tell me you caught that skunk."

Not the desired reaction. "Yup, the one that's been living in the garage. What do you think we should we do with it?"

"Well you don't want to let it go near here or it'll just come home again. Why don't you take it out to Charlene's farm and let it go?"

This sounded like a good plan, but the details were lacking. This wasn't a raccoon that would growl and pace harmlessly. This was a skunk with preemptive strike capability. How would I avoid its fragrant attack?

Maybe if I threw an old blanket over the trap the skunk would spray it and not me. I could just throw the blanket away if things went south. I didn't want it to spray my truck on the way to the farm either, but if I could place the blanket-covered trap in a little trailer and pull it behind the truck it would solve that problem. A plan with details!

I went to the garage and found an old green blanket that we used as a wrap when moving furniture. If I held it up in front of me like a bullfighter with his cape, I could approach the cage with protection and stealth.

I opened the blanket, held it up in front of me, and slowly approached the cage. So far, so good. I dropped the blanket over the cage and backed up. No sweat. Next, I drove the truck up to Bill Lukhart's house and attached his old farm trailer to the hitch and pulled it home. Slowly I placed the blanket-covered prize in the trailer. I then threw in a tomato stake that was in the garage, so that I could open the trap from a distance. I jumped in the truck and was on my way to Charlene's.

At the back end of Charlene's farm there's a gravel lane that looked like a good place to release the skunk quickly so that I could get back to town, and to work. I pulled up the lane, got out of the truck, lifted the blanket-draped trap out of the trailer, and placed it on the ground. Lifting the blanket off the top like a chef uncovering his proud creation, I backed up a few feet to check out my passenger's attitude. The skunk seemed calm enough, so I approached and released the trap doors with the tomato stake. It waddled off without even looking back. This was too easy.

"How did things go?" Susie asked as I walked into the office.

"Like clockwork. No trouble at all. I didn't get squirted and the skunk will be happier on the farm."

"You're just lucky. That could have been really bad. Maybe you ought to think twice about trapping skunks. You might have had to sleep in the camper for a few nights."

That evening, I went out to the garage to take a little motorcycle ride, and when I opened the door, I heard little feet running. This couldn't be the same skunk. It was miles away. I got the flashlight and looked under the truck. I was amazed to see another skunk! This one was a little fancier, with a black stripe down a mostly white body. I went in to report my find to Susie.

"There's another skunk in the garage—this time it's a white one," I said.

"There must be a family of them. What are we going to do?"

"Same as yesterday. I'll set the trap tonight with more bologna."

The next morning, I had caught another skunk, but to my surprise, it was not the white one. I repeated the matador routine, and took this one out to Charlene's too. No sweat.

I set the trap again that night in the hope of catching the white one. The next morning, another skunk was in the trap, this time a fancy black one with a broken white line down its back.

Every night for nine nights I caught a skunk in the trap. No two skunks looked alike. One night I caught a double! Two young siblings must have gotten a whiff of bologna simultaneously and raced for the prize. Ten for nine and never sprayed once. I'll put that record up against any professional skunk catcher's.

After the third skunk, I had had to start taking them to different farms. No sense in Charlene having the whole collection. Let's see, who needs a skunk today? I would think with each new capture. They could almost be thought of as weapons. Maybe I could put one in Henry Cashman's mailbox, the one that Bill used to load with snakes. I had a few friends who might need a skunk released near their garage. While it was fun to consider, the truth is that they all waddled into friendly woods around the county.

Fellow Rotarians began to call me Skunkbuster. Then an odd thing happened. A stranger called the office and asked to speak to the skunkbuster: Would I come out to the house and get rid of a skunk under the porch? How did he even know about this? Surely he wasn't seriously thinking that I moonlighted as a skunk catcher. Where would he get an idea like that?

That night, in the *Hillsboro Daily Times* classifieds, I read:

Skunk Trouble?
Call Skunkbusters
393-2224

This was *my* phone number that someone had put in the paper. I think I know who did it. This isn't over yet.

(No, I haven't caught the white one, but when I do. . . .)

Tough Guy

Cheryl Nickel came into the office with something small wrapped in a towel. She looked distressed.

"Dr. Sharp, I found this kitten in the road. Will you put him to sleep? He's been hit by a car or something and is really badly hurt." She opened the towel and a tiny kitten about four weeks old screamed hello.

His right rear leg had most of its skin missing. Bones were protruding above and below his knee, and his foot was gone. One eye was closed and his nose was bloody. The only part that was working well was his mouth. What a voice!

He was very young, badly hurt, probably unowned, and unquestionably in pain. A reasonable candidate for euthanasia, which was the presenter's request. But he had attitude. Cats didn't get a reputation for having nine lives by giving up easily. "Cheryl, can I keep him here and see if we can help him? I hate to put him to sleep without at least giving him a chance. Let's put him in the incubator and give him something to eat."

"He's all yours, Doc. Just don't call me if he lives. I have five cats already."

I plugged in our infant incubator, salvaged from a hospital trash pile, and picked out a can of tuna-flavored cat food (the smellier, the better). He and the tuna went in together. Only he came out. He ate the tuna until his stomach looked like a tom-tom. Bloody nose or not, this kitten liked to eat. He hadn't been asking for sympathy; he had been asking for dinner.

Further examination revealed that, aside from his obvious problem with his right rear leg, he couldn't bear weight on his right front leg either. We took whole-body x-rays, and all seemed to be well otherwise, except for a broken right elbow.

The kitten ate and rested, purring constantly. The next day we amputated what was left of his right rear leg. He woke up from the anesthesia and started to meow. We gave him a can of turkey cat food and he was purring again while he ate.

He had trouble walking after surgery, which is unusual for a cat, and the broken elbow was probably the reason. His right front leg actually seemed to get in the way. A few days passed and our kitten was gaining weight like a feeder pig. He was almost up to a pound and loved to be fed and held, but his right front leg still would not bear weight. A neurologic exam of the leg was chilling. He had no feeling anywhere below his shoulder. He didn't just have a broken elbow, he had a brachial plexus avulsion. The nerves coming out of the spinal cord that gave sensation and movement to his leg had been pulled out like a lamp plug out of a wall socket. His leg would never work again. We all felt terrible. All of us were already attached to the little guy with the big mouth.

The kitten could walk, but he would fall over his leg like it was a hurdle. What if it were not in his way? One week after amputating his right rear leg, we amputated his right front leg.

The word "amputate" is repulsive to most of us humans. We think about the consequences only in human terms: I won't be able to get a date. I won't be able to play sports. I'll never play the piano again. I'll be ugly. I've had people tell me that they would rather see their pet (companion animal, if you prefer) dead than missing a leg. Maybe they should think again.

Animals in general couldn't care less. Our kitten woke up from the anesthesia and didn't ask how he looked. He once again asked, What's for dinner?

The amputation removed a real obstacle to his recovery. He could now walk without a dead leg in his way. He had a little trouble on slippery surfaces, like a waxed floor. At first.

My son, Reid, liked to take "Lefty" out in the backyard to practice walking. He would take four or five steps and crouch down. Pretty soon he could hop across the yard. By the end of the week, Reid was afraid he could run away, since he could no longer catch him. Lefty had learned to run.

We made the brave little eating machine our practice cat, and most people who saw him didn't know that he was "disabled." He grew strong and learned to use his tail like a kick stand when he stopped. He was Lefty, and proud of it.

After eight months, he weighed ten pounds. For perspective, the average cat weighs about eight pounds, and this "average" cat has four legs. Lefty was definitely above average. He liked to lie on the windowsill with his legs hanging over the edge, like one of those half-cat ceramic shelf decorations with two hanging legs. Often, he would run out to the waiting room and down the back hall as if he were chasing some imaginary prey. He was a happy, well-adjusted cat, with no obvious disability.

Melanie Robertson and her husband cleaned our office on weekends. They had two small daughters who came along and played with Lefty while their parents worked. The girls loved him.

One morning, Melanie came in and asked to speak with me. We went into an exam room.

"What's going to happen to Lefty?" she asked.

"I thought we'd just keep him as the office cat. I don't think anyone but us would really want a cat with two legs."

Almost as if she were ashamed to say it, Melanie looked at the floor and softly said, "We do."

And so Lefty found a home. A good home with kids who love him and don't care that he's a little different.

Aren't we all?

Continuing
Education

The x-rays showed that the pelvis of the little dog was broken in at least twelve places. His major bones had been crushed when the car tire passed over his back half. I looked across the exam table at the elderly woman who was obviously upset by my description of the problem. Then came the bottom line: "I can't fix your puppy, Mrs. Reid. The university or an orthopedic specialist may be able to repair these fractures with special equipment but it's beyond my capability."

"Will it cost a lot if I decide to go to a specialist, Dr. Sharp?"

"Probably over a thousand dollars."

"I really can't afford that. Do we have any other options?"

"I suppose we could put him to sleep."

She looked at the pup and back at me and thought for a while. Then her answer surprised me. "I think I'll just take him home with me like this."

Three weeks later Mrs. Reid and the pup both walked into the office. "Look at him, Dr. Sharp! Isn't he doing well? I thought we should get him some vaccinations." His bones were healing without veterinary intervention. In school we were taught how to *fix* problems and not how to watch them go untreated. In this case I was given a lesson in time and patience.

Every day our education continues, and it often comes from unconventional teachers. Ingenuity, faith, perseverance, humility, loyalty, and patience are hard to learn in a classroom, but they can be taught to us by animals, and sometimes by their owners.

The next stories contain lessons not learned at formal meetings but rather in the school of practical truth.

All You Can Eat

"Cat" Greathouse was a mountain of a cat. He weighed over twenty-five pounds and was as white as Moby Dick. He was not all fat either. He was long, tall, and heavy-boned. When he walked, the earth moved.

His owner was a frail little woman who doted on him and provided for his every wish. He was spoiled and everyone knew it. He was brought into Dr. Ray Peters's office on a large pink cushion, like the royal pet he was.

Ray was my mentor and friend when I was a veterinary student. He had been a charter pilot before he went to vet school, and was now in practice in Columbus. One day, while I was eating lunch at the university airport, hanging out in surroundings familiar from my previous job instead of with vet students, I was introduced to Ray by the airport manager. Ray was hanging out there too. When he learned that I was a vet student and ex-Air Force, he asked me to come to his office for a visit. We talked about flying both small and large planes. He loved to fly and couldn't get enough stories about heavy jets and Vietnam combat missions, and I loved to hear him tell stories about charter flying in prop planes. After that, we had lunch at the airport and walked the hangers as often as possible. Because of my time in graduate school and the Air Force, I was a late bloomer as a vet student, only two years younger than Ray. We became immediate friends. I spent as much time as I could at his veterinary practice, and he became my preceptor, or professional schoolmaster. Veterinary medicine was a common thread, but flying was our immutable bond.

Cat had been a patient of Ray's since he'd been a little kitten. Actually, he was never a little kitten; he weighed almost three pounds when he got his first shots. Cat's weight was a subject of discussion at every visit. This time, he was brought in on his royal pillow for an extended social call. Ray had agreed to board Cat for two weeks while Mrs. Greathouse had surgery. Ray didn't board animals, but Cat was a special case, and Mrs. Greathouse was a special client.

"Now you know, Ray, that Cat will only eat shrimp. We've tried everything, but he only eats shrimp."

"I'll tell you what, Virginia, when you pick him up I'll have transformed him into a cat that will eat cat food. No more of this shrimp business. It's just not healthy for him. I'll get him eating something more normal. It'll be easier on your budget, too."

"Just be nice to my baby, Ray. Don't starve the little darling."

Cat was placed in the royal suite in the surgical prep area, where we could play with him a little during the day, and a can of fancy chicken cat food was placed in a stainless bowl in his cage, along with the usual bowl of water. The big guy turned up his nose at something that I would have eaten. It smelled wonderful.

Day two . . . canned beef cat food. No luck.

Day three . . . canned tuna cat food. No luck.

Day four . . . canned sardines in pure olive oil. No luck.

"I think tomorrow I'll bring something from home that he can't resist. That'll break the shrimp habit for sure," Ray postulated.

Day five . . . Grandma Peters's chicken and noodle casserole. No luck.

"Don't you think we ought to get him a couple of shrimp and mix them in just to get him started?" I asked.

"No, by God. He's going to learn to eat regular food!"

Day six . . . a leftover roast beef and gravy portion from the House of Sirloin. No luck.

Day seven . . . halibut from the cooler at Kroger. No luck.

Day eight . . . salmon croquettes made the old-fashioned way. No luck.

Day nine . . . dry cat food, just in case. No luck.

"Ray, do you think we ought to weigh him to see if he's lost weight while he's been 'fasting'?" I asked.

"I'll bet he could go for a month on all that reserve he's built up. But let's check."

We put Cat on the scale and he weighed in at a slim, trim 26.2 pounds. "My God, I think he's gained weight," Ray said.

Day ten . . . a five-bowl smorgasbord of chicken,

salmon, Italian meat balls, scrod, and tuna. "He's gotta like one of these." Wrong.

Day eleven, and only three days to go in the "retraining" . . . $8 worth of scallops from the Big Bear Store in Powell, Ohio. Nope.

"I can't believe this cat won't eat scallops. He's a shrimp eater. Why wouldn't he eat scallops?" Ray asked, and unknowingly answered his own question. Ray was about to lose the contest of wills.

"Let's get him some shrimp, Ray. I think he's won."

"One more try."

Day twelve . . . liver paté from the luncheon of the Friday Club. No luck.

On day thirteen, I stopped at Long John Silver's seafood restaurant on my way to Ray's office and bought an order of popcorn shrimp. We placed the shrimp in a bowl and put them in with Cat. He stood up, stretched like a chess player finished with a long match, walked over to the bowl and ate.

Ray looked over at me and said, "Do you believe that?"

Mrs. Greathouse came to retrieve Cat the next day. She brought a plastic bag with a few shrimp in it, and asked if he had been a good boy. Of course we said yes. We didn't lie.

Cat taught me a valuable lesson while he was visiting with Ray. The military uses the philosophy: Your mom's not cooking for you here, boys. Eat it or don't eat it. It's up to you. You can apply this to dogs, since they will eventually eat when they get hungry. It might take a day or two or three, but dogs (and humans) will eventually throw in the towel and eat what they're served. Cats may not. Cat Greathouse did not. In a battle of wills, a cat might prevail.

I also learned a lot from Ray during the years following—

when I worked as his student assistant. Most of the routine procedures that I do today, I learned from Ray. He also served as a daily example in his manner of dealing with people. His caring attitude and kind approach to owners was not something you could learn from a textbook. As a result, he was a veterinarian with a devoted group of clients. He had his first heart attack at the age of thirty-two, and when he returned to work, a remarkable number of his clients hugged him when he walked into the exam room. We even talked about practicing together, but it never happened. He had his last heart attack when he was thirty-seven.

It's been more than twenty years now and I think of Ray often. He aimed a veterinary student in the right direction, and I'll be forever grateful. All because of the chance meeting of two guys who liked to fly.

Friends

Bob and Molly were my only Pike County horse clients. My trips to their farm were always more social than professional. I went to treat the horses, but enjoyed the companionship of the owners so much that it never seemed like work. I would not have traveled an hour into another county if I hadn't enjoyed myself.

They owned three hundred acres of southern Ohio wooded hills that were crisscrossed with riding trails. Occasional ponds were scattered among the green pastures and woods. The house was modern, decorated with Native American art, and boasted an indoor sauna and hot tub. A four-car garage, an eight-stall horse barn, a riding arena, and a swimming pool were all tucked away at the end of a long lane that hid all of this from the road. It was a horse-lover's paradise, and if you didn't like horses, they had three Corvettes. Real horsepower.

The farm was beautiful, but it was the owners that made the trip worthwhile. Bob was a Marine veteran of D-Day and had built the barn himself. Molly was a competition-oriented equestrienne with a wall of trophies. The fact that they were in their seventies neither slowed them down nor altered their outlook. They lived at full throttle and were a pleasure to be near. After treating the horses, we always went into the house for coffee and conversation. Occasionally my office would call to see where I had strayed.

On this October day, it was not a horse that had a problem. Melissa stuck her head in the exam-room door. "Dr. Sharp, Bob Buschagen just called on his cell phone and they're on their way in with Asta. He just backed his horse trailer over her head." Asta was one of the four family dogs that played on the farm. She was an Airedale and Bob's favorite.

I quickly completed the vaccination of the dog that was already on the exam table. I then went to the treatment area to get equipment and drugs ready for Asta. "Where was Bob when he called?" I asked Melissa.

"Just passing through Marshall, about fifteen minutes away."

"He could be here anytime," I said as the door burst open and Bob came in carrying a limp Asta. He must have rocketed through town.

"I can't believe I did this to her. We'd just finished loading the horses and I was backing up just a few feet to pull out of the lane. I pulled ahead and saw her in the rear-view mirror lying in the gravel. She must have been back there and I never saw her."

"Put her down here on the table, Bob, and let's take a look." She was unconscious and bleeding from both ears. Her eyes were rolled back in her head and her gums were very pale. As we started treatment for shock, Bob sat down and put his head in his hands.

Her head was injured most severely, and she had a few cuts from the gravel on her elbows. While the fluids and drugs were dripping through IV lines into both front legs, I examined her head wounds a little more thoroughly. The top of her head was swollen already and I thought I could feel cracks in the bone. The bony arch over her right eye was broken. Her nose was broken and bleeding and her jaw was split in the middle with broken teeth sticking through a hole in her lip. If she lived, which was doubtful, she would need some orthopedic work.

"Bob, why don't you go on to the horse show and leave Asta with me. It doesn't look very good, but there's nothing you can do here."

"Rob, you know how I feel about this dog. Spare no expense. If she needs something, give it to her. All I want is my Asta back. I can't believe I did this to her."

I stayed with Asta until late into the evening. Her blood pressure improved and her gums became pink again, but she had not regained consciousness and brain swelling was a probability. I went home expecting that she would be dead the next time I saw her. About 2 AM I went back to the office to check on her, and was surprised that she was alive. She had not moved; she was unconscious, but alive.

The next morning came early. I opened the office door,

again expecting that Asta would be dead. She was not. Still out cold, not moving, barely breathing, but alive. I rolled her over on her blanket so that she would spend equal time on each side. Radiographs of her skull revealed more fractures than I had expected. Cracks radiated across the top of her skull like spokes of a bike wheel. Her jaw was broken in several places. This dog would probably never regain consciousness.

Bob called from the horse show daily and was never given very good news. She was alive, but not responding. Without anesthesia, I repaired her broken jaw. She couldn't be aware of any pain. A week after her injury, Bob and Molly stopped in for a visit. Asta was thin and not responding. They didn't want to discuss euthanasia. Where there's life. . . .

I had earlier inserted a stomach tube to give her some nutrition, and that night, when I patted her back after feeding her, she wagged her tail. I couldn't get to the phone fast enough to call her owners. It was only a tail wag but it was a sign of recognition. The lightbulbs were beginning to light. Maybe she wasn't hopeless after all.

Each day for the next week we worked on the tail wag. We spoke to her constantly and kept her in the treatment area so that we could pat her back and get a response whenever we walked by. We were happy to pester her. She seemed to like it too.

The next week, Asta began to move her mouth, and with a little help holding her head, she could lap water. Her eyes remained closed but her improvement was obvious.

She recognized her master's voice and her tail would wave a welcome when she heard him come for a visit. We would take turns sitting on the floor, holding her head while she drank her dog-food soup. After three weeks, she could not even roll over; she was becoming a rack of bones and atrophied muscles, developing bedsores in spite of constant care, but we could not give up. She was awakening daily.

We used our large stainless steel sink as a bathtub, both for therapy and hygiene. After almost drowning her on one attempt we developed a method of head support that seemed safe. Daily baths helped her ulcers heal. She was no longer a patient. She had become a friend and a challenge. To greet us in the mornings, she wagged her tail and howled like a coonhound. Asta would not give up. How could we?

We went through a routine of helping her swim in the tub, helping her eat, eventually helping her to sit up, and after four months, we helped her stand. On February 1, she took her first step.

All of our regular clients knew Asta. She had been visited by people who had never known her before her injury. By March, she could walk without assistance, and it was time to go home. It took her five minutes of deliberate effort to walk to Bob's truck for the ride to Pike County and her beautiful farm. She and Bob were so very happy.

I called a few days later to see how things were going and was pleased to hear that Asta was walking around the house and the horse arena and gaining in strength and coordination daily.

Spring had arrived, bringing flowers, warmth, and ticks. Dogs were getting into trouble and the practice was very busy. One afternoon, in the middle of office hours, Bob

Buschagen came to see me. Melissa said he wanted to talk to me in private, so we went into an exam room.

Bob gave me his Marine Corps handshake, but without the usual smile. "I'd rather be anywhere than here with you now, Rob."

"Why?" I asked, noticing that tears had been wiped from his cheeks.

"Asta was getting along wonderfully. She was even playing with the other dogs and acting like her old self. The dogs went down to the pond and she went with them. Rob, she could walk, but apparently she couldn't swim. I found her in the pond lilies this morning. I'm so sorry." He sat down and put his head in his hands again.

Asta taught me patience. She taught me that no matter how hopeless a case appears, recovery may be possible. Most important, she reminded me how dogs can serve as examples of how to behave when we are miserable. How to wag a tail.

We buried Asta in our hearts.

Big Mouth

Some wounds are uglier than others. When I look at a wound, I think about what needs to be done to fix it. Owners think of something else. An animal will be injured and go home. There were no human witnesses, and no amount of thought will tell you how the injury happened. The animal may have a broken bone, and the first question the owner will ask is never, "Can you fix it?" or, "What will it cost?" or even, "Will he live?" The first question is always the one you can't answer: "Gee, Doc, how did she do that?" We could be thinking that the dog in question was hit by a car, when in truth he broke his leg sliding under a manure spreader while chasing his arch-enemy, Twinkles the rat terrier. I have asked animals how they hurt themselves, but they're usually ashamed to answer. It rarely matters. Lacerations are sutured, abscesses are drained, fractures are repaired, and the secret remains: "Gee, Doc, how did she do that?"

Henry the collie had a really ugly wound. His hair was stuck to it, and once we clipped the hair away, the wound was even uglier. The skin on his right rear leg above the knee was black and dead in an area about four inches in diameter. Some pus was visible under the dark skin. It was obviously an abscess that had begun developing days before. Probably a bite wound from a dog, or cat, or groundhog, or whatever. Then the bacteria that were injected by the teeth multiplied over the next few days. The immune system responded, and dead white cells, dead bacteria, and other debris littered Henry's biological battlefield. Pus, for short. The pressure and heat of battle caused the skin circulation in the area to be disrupted, and the covering skin died. A hole developed and the pus drained out sticking to the hair. A real mess. The dead skin would need to be removed so that healing could occur. It was ugly but not a difficult problem in this time of good antibiotics.

"Gosh, Doc, what do you think caused it?" said Mrs. Selmons.

"Judging by the dead skin and the progress of the abscess, I'd say a bite was inflicted about four or five days ago."

"No way! He was fine this morning." Time is a relative thing and handled carelessly by some folks. If an animal is to be euthanized, it becomes much older than it really is. If an animal is injured, it just happened. This makes the owner feel better. People like to justify their action, or lack of it.

It was impossible for this to have happened to Henry on this morning. Impossible. Pus doesn't appear in the wink of an eye. Skin doesn't turn black while you drink your morning coffee. The dog was not "fine this morning." Knowing this, I violated that important rule about keeping your mouth shut, a violation that my mother pointed out to me frequently both as a child and an adult. "Naw, this is pretty old. The skin's black!"

Why should I have cared what this client thought? But there's something about a situation in which your opinion is solicited and, when given, immediately contradicted, that serves up a challenge. After all, Mrs. Selmons was paying for my opinion. If she didn't want it, she shouldn't have asked.

"I'm telling you, Doc, that leg was fine this morning. The hair was perfect. The dog didn't limp. He was perfect."

This is where the debate should have stopped and the repair have begun, but I had to add one more comment. Unnecessary and probably inaccurate to boot. "The only thing I know that can cause a wound that ugly and that quickly is the necrotizing toxin of a poisonous snake." Why did I say that?

She said nothing, and looked a little pale as she handed me the leash.

"You can pick him up tomorrow after lunch," I said, watching her go out the door.

We anesthetized Henry, cleaned up the wound, gave him an injection of an antibiotic, and counted out some pills to send home with him. He would be fine and was ready to leave the next day.

The next day came and went. No Mrs. Selmons.

The day after that came and went. No Mrs. Selmons.

The next day came and went. Still no Mrs. Selmons.

"Henry, I think your mom has abandoned you," I said, hoping I was kidding.

At four PM, Mrs. Selmons walked into the waiting room.

"Hi!" I said, relieved. "I thought I was going to see you on Tuesday."

"I've been moving."

"No kidding. Did you buy a new house?" I asked.

"Nope. Me and them dogs moved in with my sister. We ain't gonna live anywhere near them damn snakes."

My mother was right.

Holey Cow

Melissa Montgomery moved to Hillsboro in 1980. She had just graduated from Columbus Technical Institute as a Registered Animal Technician. She was from Chillicothe, and applied for a job at the practice I was leaving. Lucky for me, they couldn't use her, but I could. She took the big step and moved away from home to take a chance working with a new practice owner.

The Allis Chalmers tractor dealership across the street from the office had a young tractor mechanic who would come to our office to pick up medicine for his parents' dairy herd. He and Melissa seemed to be taking longer and longer for simple transactions. The rest is history. Melissa has been married to Dale for over twenty years and has worked with me until this day. Dale's mother became my kids' babysitter, and her dairy herd was always a personal concern.

I had just finished putting an intermedullary bone pin into the broken femur of a cat one morning, when Melissa called me over to the phone. "Rob, my mother-in-law has a sick cow and doesn't know what's wrong with her. You probably have time to go out this morning if you want. A spay just canceled."

"Tell Charlene that I'll be out around noon. I'll grab a wiener at the Dairy Queen and then head over to the farm."

The Montgomery dairy farm is just a few miles outside town. They farm about 160 acres and milk about 75 Holstein cows. If needed, I could be there in ten minutes.

I drove down the long gravel lane, past the house and equipment shed, and pulled up next to the milking parlor. The huge stainless steel holding tank in the parlor was cooling down the morning milk. The truck hadn't come to pick it up yet. Charlene was still cleaning up, which takes quite a while after a herd of cows has come through the parlor.

The milking room is about the size and design of a gas-station lubrication bay. The milker works in a pit in the center, and his eyes are at udder level. Four cows come in each side of the pit at once, and face slightly outward into feed pans. Sliding doors are closed behind and in front of the eight that are being milked. A measured amount of grain drops down from above and into a pan in front of each cow. The cow eats contentedly while her udder is washed, dried, and the milkers applied. The cows are kept from falling onto the dairyman by steel rails on each side of the pit. The milk is carried to the holding tank by a series of clear plastic lines that are cleaned and sanitized after milking is finished. After one batch of cows is milked, they are sent out through the front of the parlor and eight more are let in through the back.

The cows actually line themselves up outside in the holding area, since they like to come in for some tasty grain. Some like the left side, some the right. They always come in with their friends, and in the same order. If there is a holdup, Nancy, the three-legged Australian cattle dog, encourages the recalcitrant cow with a little nip on the hock. Every cow that isn't in the dry lot awaiting the birth of a calf must be milked twice a day, every day, 365 days of the year. No vacations. No Christmas break. No hangover excuses. Every single day, rain or shine, in sickness and in health. Dairymen have one of the hardest jobs in farming.

The sick cow I'd come to see was in the holding area outside the milking parlor. "Why do you think she's sick, Charlene?" I asked.

"This morning, when she came in to be milked, she didn't eat anything. She usually milks about fifty pounds a day, and this morning she was way off on that too."

"Let's move her into the parlor and take a look at her." We slid the entrance door open and #297 walked inside, her udder swinging to and fro. We dropped a little feed in the trough and waited. No interest.

"How long has she been off her feed?"

"Just today, I'm pretty sure. We didn't notice her not eating yesterday."

I took her temperature rectally. Normal. I listened to her rumen sounds and lungs. "Is she bred, Charlene?"

"She should be about five months along, and not even close to being put out with the dry cows yet." A couple of months before a calf is due, the cow is intentionally "dried up." This allows her udder to recover and colostrum to form before the cow gives birth and milking resumes. The calf is only permitted to nurse for the first day to get colostrum, which gives the calf immunity to common cattle diseases, and is then fed milk-replacer from a bottle. On a dairy farm, the cow's milk is not for the calf. The cow will be rebred at the earliest opportunity, usually within a few weeks of delivery, and the cycle starts over.

I put on a palpation sleeve, lubed it up, and inserted my arm into her rectum. I could easily feel her uterus, and her calf was just as described. It felt like it was five or six months in size, and developing normally. I removed my arm and pulled off the sleeve.

"Let's check her for hardware," I said. Cows aren't very careful when they eat. They sometimes swallow nails, metal fragments, or anything else on the ground, which then drops into the rumen. From there, it falls into the reticulum, which is the stomach next to the diaphragm. Movement of the reticulum and the diaphragm can cause the nail to puncture the reticulum and then go through the diaphragm and actually rub the pericardium sur-rounding the heart. Traumatic reticulitis and traumatic pericarditis are usually referred to as "hardware disease." Most dairymen drop a cylindrical magnet into each cow. It stays there for the life of the cow and grabs any metal objects she happens to swallow, keeping them from punc-turing the reticulum.

"Charlene, does she have a magnet?"

"I'm pretty sure that she doesn't. I don't remember put-ting one in her."

I went back to the truck and got out my metal detector. It's almost voodoo medicine to use one of these to diagnose hardware disease since most cows, including those with a magnet, will demonstrate some metal if tested. If no metal is detected, however, it can be used to rule it out. She tested free of any metal at all. She did not have hardware disease.

I could find no reason why this cow wouldn't eat. She had a reason. I just hadn't found it.

There is a saying that for every diagnosis missed by not knowing, ten are missed by not looking. I looked. I looked in her mouth. I palpated her rectally, and I examined everything in between. I examined her thoroughly and found nothing abnormal. I could find no reason for her illness.

"I'm going to take some blood back with me and we'll send it off to the lab." If she went off her feed for long, Charlene would lose fifty pounds of milk every day. If #297 died, she would lose the cow, the unborn calf, and the milk as well. Thousands of dollars were at stake. There was no time to lose. "Treat her like a normal cow until I get the lab work back," I told Charlene, and I left some large rumen boluses with her. They would settle the cow's stomachs if she had an upset GI tract. Really just a long shot, but it might help her feel better.

"What did you find wrong with Charlene's cow?" Melissa asked when I walked into the office.

"Not a thing. She looks normal. I brought some blood back with me. Can you get it centrifuged and sent out so we'll have the results tomorrow?"

"No problem."

The next day the blood count and profile results were those of a normal, healthy cow. I called Charlene and gave her the report. "Is she eating yet?" I asked.

"Not a bit. Her milk is still dropping off too. What should we do next?"

"I'll call the cow guys at OSU and talk to them about this. They may have some ideas."

"Tell Melissa to come out for lunch today. I've made chicken and noodles. Homemade noodles. You can come too, Rob."

"Thanks, Charlene. Your noodles are the best, but I'll pass. I'll tell Melissa."

The bovine medicine instructors at Ohio State are always willing to help. I talked with Dr. Bruce Moore, who had been one of my instructors. I wanted to know if putting a window into the rumen was a reasonable idea. Food could then be placed directly into the rumen from outside the cow. This would keep her milking until the problem resolved itself. He agreed, and had done it himself with a cow that wouldn't eat for an unknown reason.

I called Charlene and told her the plan. She was up for it. We got the cow into the dry lot, tied her to a post, and prepared her left side for surgery. The incision would be on the left side, behind the ribs, right over the rumen. The rumen is the first stomach that food enters. It's as big as a sleeping bag and is filled with grass, hay, grain, and anything else the cow has eaten. This mixing chamber holds food, and churns until it drops into the next stomach, the reticulum.

I infiltrated the skin with lidocaine along the planned incision line. Then I got all the instruments ready while the lidocaine was taking effect.

When I was a kid, my dentist would give me an injection of local anesthetic and then start to drill. At about the time he was done, the tooth would get numb. I suffered silently. The cow would not. She would kick me with a lightning foot in a way that would let me know that my technique was flawed. I gave the lidocaine plenty of time to work.

I poked a needle into old #297 in the proposed incision area, and she just stood there without paying attention. The sweet smell of silage was coming out of the feed bunker next to us. Barn cats were gathering around her feet hoping for a little milk to drip from her huge udder. Cows came up to the fence to watch. Everything was ready. "Are you ready for this, #297? Let me know if you feel anything." She stood quietly and flicked a fly with her tail.

I made an eighteen-inch-long incision and cut through the thick skin. The cow felt nothing. I could easily see the rumen wall beneath the skin, and I made a similar vertical cut in it. I then stitched the left side of the rumen incision to the left side of the skin incision and did the same on the right side. When this healed, a hole would be open directly into the rumen and food could be placed inside. Really pretty simple. Pretty cool.

Dale drove up the lane and came over to see what was happening.

"Check this out," I said, holding the window open. "Go get a coffee can full of grain and let's give her a snack."

"Amazing! Look at the stuff in there. Smells like methane gas."

"Better not light a match around her. I'd hate to see her running through the dry lot with flames shooting out of her side." We dumped some grain into the rumen. Perfecto.

For the next few weeks, #297 was fed alfalfa pellets,

grain, and hay through the window in her rumen. She produced a normal amount of milk and didn't appear to lose much weight. Even when you're as big as a cow, weight loss is easily noticed.

After three weeks, Charlene called the office. "Hey Rob, how long do we have to keep dumping feed in #297?"

"Until she eats on her own," I supposed.

"Well, she came in to be milked this morning, and ate grain when I dumped it in the pan."

"Great! Let's only put about half as much hay and pellets in her rumen for a few days. Maybe she'll eat on her own if we don't feed her."

It worked like a charm. After another week she was on full feed and milking better than ever. I went out to the farm, surgically closed my window, and two weeks later removed the stitches. She delivered her calf, was milked the next year, produced several more calves over the years, and was never sick again.

To this day, I have no idea why she refused to eat.

Abandoned

Dear Compassionet Vet
this
Please do something with / cat--
cure it or kill it !
THANK YOU !

This note was attached to a bag that once contained oranges and was hung by its string on our exit door. Unfortunately, the cat was not inside the bag, but there was a hole about the size of a cat torn out of the bag's side. On the back of the note was written:

~~Compashient~~   ~~Compashinent~~
~~Compassionet~~   ~~Commpassine~~

An apparent lack of concern for the cat was offset by a concern for spelling. (The person also needed a better bag.) Abandoning an animal at a veterinarian's doorstep isn't uncommon, but it's always maddening. We walked around the office looking for a cat that needed curing or killing, but found nothing. It had escaped, and probably wouldn't be found.

This made me think of another time, twenty years ago, when a Hispanic man came into the office with a large black Labrador retriever on a rope.

"Dr. Sharp, I just got this dog at the animal shelter and I would like to have her fixed up while I'm in town. My family is here to pick apples at the area orchards, and we fell in love with her when we were at the shelter. I don't have a house here in town, so I would like to board her with you while we work, and then get her when we leave to go home."

"Where's your home?" I asked, for the sake of conversation.

"A little town in west Texas. We're up here during the harvest, and we'll go home in the winter."

"How long do you want me to board her?"

"About two weeks. Is that OK?"

"No problem, but we need to vaccinate her for her own protection."

"I would like that done anyway, and say, Doc, while she's here, can you spay her?"

"I should have time in the next week."

"My wife would like to see her, so if I bring her by, can we visit?"

"Sure, anytime." I took the rope while Melissa filled out a record with pertinent information.

A week later, the whole family came for a visit. The dog, which they named Mama, had been spayed, bathed, vaccinated, and generally spruced up, and was looking good. The three kids loved her, the husband sat on the floor with her, and the wife, who spoke only Spanish, didn't say much. "We'll be back to get her in a week, Dr. Sharp. How much will we owe you when we get her?"

Melissa calculated the bill and gave it to them.

"See you next week," they all said, as they left the office.

I'm still waiting for their return. We found a home for Mama within the month. She was a wonderful family dog, and for many years made her owners thankful that she had been abandoned.

Several valuable lessons were learned in this episode (one of which was that I probably should have suspected something when he said his name was Smith).

At least the people who dropped off the cat left a note with their intentions. The office staff discussed the kind of humans who would leave a cat in a bag, and decided that the people probably couldn't afford to fix it, but were still well intentioned. Not knowing what their situation was, I thought that they might have been doing the best they could; at least they didn't dump her by the roadside. But it did turn out that way. The day's work progressed.

My son, who came to work at the office after school, went out in front of the building to water the flower boxes. He returned with a question: "Are you guys aware that there's a cat sitting in the flower box by the exit door? Her eyes are stuck shut and are really gross."

"Sounds like a cat that needs killing or curing," I said.

"What are you talking about?" the high school sophomore asked.

I showed him the note as I went out to the flower box. There, huddled up under a big red geranium, was a beautiful little calico cat. Her nostrils were plugged with crusty green goo, and her eyes were plastered shut. I picked her up and carried her into the office.

"She was only about a foot from the doorknob. She must have climbed out of the bag and stopped there. I can't believe we didn't see her. Let's soak her eyelids open and see what things look like under there."

She had the standard respiratory infection common to barn cats that aren't vaccinated, and the secondary bacterial infection that follows. Two weeks on amoxicillin and eye drops, and she was ready for a cat show. We tested her for the bad viruses: Feline Leukemia, FIV, and FIP, and when we were satisfied that she was healthy, I called a client who was a particularly easy target. A little talk about abuse, a little salesmanship, and a veiled threat of not being able to find a home, and our drop-off was leading the good life, riding with three other cats in a white Jaguar sedan. From an orange net bag to tan leather in two weeks. We were happy for her.

Not long ago, someone tied two obviously purebred German shepherds to the front porch posts of the office with a Gordian knot. I guess this was better than throwing them out of the car somewhere in the country, and now we would have to start the usual procedures for finding a home for them. Maybe they had a home and got lost, and were then found by the people who tied them to our posts. Maybe they had a home and were evicted by the people who'd left them. They could at least have left a note telling us the dogs' history.

We might find the shepherds' owners, or find some new owners for them, but until then, we'll feed them and take care of them. The usual phone calls have been made, and we won't have them for long.

Since the business across the street has installed security cameras that can also see our building, we now have a new tool to help us with these drop-offs. The truck that brought these dogs and left them here might be identified. Dumping animals is against the law.

I can't remember, over the years, how many animals have appeared without an owner to care for them. And last year, a new variation of the drop-off problem reared its head.

Late in the fall a young woman came into the office with a handful of coarse straw-colored hair with eyes.

"I found this in the road, and when I went up to the nearby house to tell them that their puppy had escaped and was in the road, the woman said that she knew it. She had a bunch of them, and this one had already had a broken leg."

The pup on the table looked like an unmade bed. She weighed less than two pounds, had tan hair pointing in every direction, and watched every move that I made. "What breed of dog is this?" I asked.

"The woman said she was purebred, and she sold them, so I bought her. I don't know what breed. Will you break her leg and straighten it like the other one?"

Her right radius and ulna had been broken and had healed with her foot pointing a little bit outward. "I think that would be a bad idea. She already walks on this, and it healed in a pretty usable position. If we break it, we may do nerve or blood-vessel damage. Her leg is so small, it may not heal. We might make it a lot worse than it is now."

"Then I'm going to take her back. I wanted to sell her, and I can't if her leg is crooked. I don't even want you to vaccinate her. That's just throwing good money after bad."

Susie, my wife, was walking by the exam room and heard the woman's comment. She walked in, picked up the two-pound orphan, and said, "How much do you want for her?"

"A hundred dollars."

My own wife, without batting an eye, said "OK."

I stood by with my mouth open and watched as my wife paid a hundred dollars for a stray dog with a broken leg.

As is true of most veterinarians, our own animals are all former orphans—ones that are missing body parts, require constant treatment, or have some deformity that makes them unacceptable to some people. I now had another one.

"Twinkie" weighs only three pounds, even today. She goes with me to elementary schools when I am a guest, and kids love her. She still looks like an unmade bed, but she's my constant pal and the best hundred bucks we ever spent.

I'm sure this new twist on the "abandon the animal at the vet's office" routine was unintentional. But it did work like a charm. As for Susie—P. T. Barnum was right.

CSI Hillsboro

Amy, our daughter, was in kindergarten when we moved to Hillsboro. The next year, she became a Brownie, and Susie, of course, became a Brownie leader. Brownie leaders work in teams and the other mother to volunteer was Jenny Harris. They planned activities for the weekly meetings, went on field trips, camped, and led the girls through the flying-up ceremony into Girl Scouts. Susie and Jenny had a lot of fun with the girls and stayed on as Girl Scout leaders. Jenny's husband, Jim, and I were occasional helpers with construction and carrying of ceremonial paraphernalia. He and I became friends.

One September morning I was finishing our fourth scheduled surgery and things were going along without a hitch when Jim walked into the office through the exit door. He walked back to the treatment area carrying a dog.

"I just found Ralph lying under the bridge that crosses the creek back on the farm. He's dead. Rob, I wonder if you can help me find out what happened to him?"

"Put him on the sink and I'll take a look in just a second." I put the last sutures in Killer Markle's castration incision, took off my gloves, and went over to the big stainless steel sink. Ralph was an eighty-pound mixed breed farm dog. He was a big, gentle dog that never left the 260 acres of woods and fields of his home.

"His head feels very soft and squishy, Jim. Like there's no bone in it. Something's crushed his skull. What do you think happened to him? Could he have been hit by a car?"

"He was back off the road by our tenant's house. Two hundred yards from the road, and under the little bridge down in the water. He wasn't on the porch for breakfast this morning, so the girls went out looking for him. I went to work, and Jenny called a half hour ago and said the twins had found him. I went home, picked him up and put him in the truck, and brought him right here. The girls are really upset."

Jim owned a car dealership in town and was dressed in a business suit that was now soaking wet with creek water.

"Why don't we take some x-rays and see if we can find something on film," I proposed. "Just leave him with me and we'll work on it while you go home and change clothes. Give me until this afternoon and call me around three. We ought to have something by then."

"Thanks, Rob. I'll have to get his body this evening."

Melissa and I carried Ralph's body over to the x-ray table. I wanted to look at his skull first. The cassettes were placed under his head and we donned our lead aprons and lead gloves. We took both lateral and dorsoventral views so that we could see in three dimensions. Melissa developed the films while I examined the rest of Ralph's body.

I could find no wound on any part other than the head, and I knew that the radiographs would tell the story.

"They're in the water," Melissa announced.

I held the dripping films up to the light box and saw the bright radiopaque perfect outline of an undamaged bullet and the resulting shattered skull. The entry wound was on the top of the head and the trajectory was straight down from above. Someone had executed Ralph.

We see gunshot wounds more often than I'd like. It's unusual to see a bullet that isn't deformed after hitting a bone, though. Usually a dog is shot when it's chasing sheep, getting into a herd of cattle, barking below a poacher's deer stand, or engaged in a variety of lesser transgressions. I repair a lot of gunshot fractures, and the bullet is usually badly deformed or powdered after hitting bone. Most dogs are shot with a high velocity, .22-caliber center-fire round that disintegrates on impact. The classic groundhog rifle. The bullet in Ralph was not a .22-caliber round.

One of the sports that I've enjoyed and practiced over the last fifteen years is trap shooting. If you shoot trap a lot, you shoot a lot of shotgun shells. The empty hulls of the fired shells can be recycled or reloaded to be used again. As a result, I own all the equipment needed to accurately measure and weigh powder and bullets.

I removed the bullet from Ralph and took it back to my loading bench. The bullet weighed 71 grains, was round-nosed, and covered with a metal jacket. It was .311 inches in diameter. This is a perfect match for a .32-caliber handgun cartridge. Ralph was shot at close range with a small-caliber pistol. An unusual caliber to boot. I called Jim at the dealership and gave him my report.

"Thanks, Rob. The sheriff and I will be out later to get Ralph and the evidence. I think I know who did this and we'll be going out to talk to him."

That night, after supper and a short motorcycle ride down the Belfast Pike and home again, I was sitting on the porch when the phone rang.

"Hi, Rob. This is Jim Harris. I thought that you'd be interested in what happened this afternoon."

"Did you get the bad guy?"

"Sure did. I thought my tenant had done this since his house is a baseball pitch from the bridge. What a dummy. We pulled up in front of his house in the cruiser and the sheriff and I went up on the porch. He came out, wearing dirty jeans and no shirt. In his most official tone Jerry asked him 'Do you own a .32 caliber handgun?' He said that he did. Then he asked him if he had shot a big dog, and he said that he had!"

"I asked him why he would shoot a dog that wasn't doing anything wrong, and he said, 'no good reason.' So next, I asked him if he knew the dog was mine. He said no. Then I asked him where he planned to live next month because it wasn't going to be on my place."

"What did the sheriff do?" I asked.

"He took him to his office to press charges. I'm not sure what charges yet. I think Jerry wants to throw the book at him. Thanks again for your help with this, Rob."

Jim sent me a one-twelfth-scale factory model of a 1953 Corvette and signed it "from Ralph."

That wasn't the only time we've been asked to assign blame in a shooting.

Billy Jackson's black-and-tan coonhound was brought to the office one day in the back of a pickup. He had come home the previous evening and dropped dead on the back porch. Billy found him and suspected foul play. He thought that his neighbor, a sheep farmer, had shot him.

"I want you to do an autopsy on him, Doc, and find out what happened. My neighbor has threatened to shoot him if he found him in his sheep. Flash might go over there, but he's just going to the woods looking for 'coons. Save the bullet for proof," he said.

We took radiographs, and Flash had indeed been shot. Not once, but three times. There was no doubt as to the cause of death. Since Bill asked for an autopsy (really necropsy, since autopsy means "to dissect oneself" and is reserved for the dissection of humans), I did take a look at all of Flash's organs and found a surprise. Inside his stomach was a double handful of wool. Flash had indeed been chasing sheep, and catching them, too.

Billy came back for the body and the proof. I showed him the radiographs, and he was mad. I showed him the plastic bag full of wool, and he was crestfallen. "Looks like I owe the man some money and an apology. I never would have believed it of Flash."

Poachers have been known to break the law and try to outsmart the game warden. Rifles are not used for deer hunting in Ohio. There is shotgun season and primitive-weapon season. Both of these weapons fire relatively short-range projectiles, limiting the possibility of hitting the wrong target three miles away, as a rifle bullet can.

John Davis, who is our area state game protector, came into the office with a problem. "Doc, we think this deer was taken illegally," he said, pointing to a buck in the back of his truck. "Can we take an x-ray of him?"

"Sure, what part do you want to look at? We can see 14 inches by 17 inches at a time."

"His neck. This guy that we suspect is from out of the county, and he said he shot this buck in the Tranquility Wildlife Area. He says he brought him down with the arrow that's in him. Can we look in there and see what really happened?"

"Let's get him inside and on the x-ray table. Three of us can carry him, can't we?"

"I think so. Jimmy's in the truck and can help."

We lifted the big buck out of the back of the truck and carried his stiff body back to the x-ray table. An arrow had entered the left side of his neck and was exiting the right side, razor point still attached.

"You know, John, this arrow didn't hit the carotid artery

or jugular vein on either side, and it didn't hit the spine. It doesn't look like a fatal shot. I would think that a buck this size would just keep on running with the arrow sticking out. Pretty gross, though."

"That's what Larry at the check-in station thought, too. He called me after locking up the deer."

A lateral view of the neck showed that the deer had indeed been brought down by a single shot to his neck, but not from a bow. A rifle bullet had entered one side of the neck, hit the spinal column, bringing down the buck, and then bounced twenty degrees downward and made an exit wound lower down on the opposite side of his neck—lower than a straight line through the neck because of deflection off the bone. Lead fragments were all over his spine. The dummy had pushed a hunting arrow in the entry wound, and across the neck to the exit wound. This arrow-straight line was suspicious, because it was not a killing shot. He forgot about the deflection, and he forgot about the law. Case closed.

While You Were Out . . .

The bishop's robe was as white as marshmallow creme, and flowed to the ground in front of me, so close that I could touch it. I had been kneeling for what seemed like an eternity while the Episcopal service of Holy Communion continued. It was an honor to have the bishop conducting the service in our little parish, and an honor to be his acolyte. But even a high school kid's knees have a limit. He spoke slowly and reverently, and a good long service was the result. The next thing I remember was a close-up view of his shoelaces and the bass man from the choir asking if I was all right. I was dragged unceremoniously to one of the ornate chairs that decorated the altar and told to put my head between my knees. I had fainted. Just imagine my embarrassment. I had taken a nose dive into the bishop's shoes right in the middle of a prayer. In front of God and my mother.

Funny thing, this fainting. You never know when it might hit you, and often don't know why. The ancients must have been mystified by it too, since a term was constructed for it that sounds almost like something from a seance: "passing out." Veterinarians are forced to deal with this mysterious phenomenon with some regularity, and a few cases come to mind.

Melissa had worked for me for several years before she got to assist in a caesarian delivery of pups. Caesarians always seemed to be needed at night, and so I did the surgeries without help. Sometimes the owner would help with the pups once they had been delivered, but even that was rare. Most people preferred to read a magazine in the waiting room and leave the work to me. Or they went home and said "Call me in the morning, Doc."

One night, Gracie Anderson's bulldog, Jellybean, was in labor and, as is the custom of bulldogs, giving it no real effort at all. A C-section was needed. Tonight I'll have some real help! I thought, as I started to get out all of the instrument packs and equipment. Gracie was a surgical nurse at our local hospital and spent her days assisting in surgery. There was no limit to what she could do. She could get injectable drugs and administer them, she could get additional instruments and supplies ready during surgery, and even give anesthesia if needed. She could do all those things that would otherwise slow me down, and she had done it all before.

We discussed the surgery as Jellybean was going to sleep, and talked about similarities and differences in human procedure. I put Jelly on the table, tied her to the table cleats, clipped her abdomen, scrubbed it with surgical soap, wiped it with alcohol, and then put on my gloves. I took one last look around for anything that I might have forgotten, checked on the sleeping bulldog, and put sterile drapes around the area of the incision. As I attached the #10 blade to the scalpel, I asked Gracie if she would like to stand on the other side of the surgery table for a better view. And so she stood in her usual position, opposite the surgeon.

I began with a skin incision about six inches long, and as I reached for a gauze sponge, I saw Gracie lean back against the wall. Her face was as white as a bishop's robes, and she was going down. I circled the table, grabbed her before her head hit the floor, and propped her up against the cabinets. My hopes for help had just bitten the dust.

I went to the refrigerator, got out a Diet Pepsi, and put it on the floor next to Gracie. When she came to, she was as amazed as I was that this had happened. "I've never done that before in my entire life!" she said in disbelief. She watches surgery every day, but this time it was a "family member."

Our local schools want kids to be exposed to some occupations before they make their career choices when they're seniors. Veterinary medicine is a popular choice, so on "job shadowing" day we used to allow schoolkids to come to the office. But we made too many sick. One day, five eighth-graders came in the morning to job shadow during our surgery time. Three fainted, one threw up, and one watched from the room across the hall. Contagious fainting? We now have shadowers come in the afternoon to watch our scheduled appointments—and no surgery.

Another day, a trucker who came to pick up his rottweiler that had just had a broken leg repaired passed out when he looked at the x-rays. No blood, no guts, just radiographs in an air-conditioned room. Have you ever tried to catch a 270-pound truck driver on his way to the floor? Me neither. It wasn't pretty.

One of the stranger episodes of this mysterious behavior happened on a cold night in November. I had rushed to the office to see a beagle with trouble having puppies.

The little female looked up at me from the treatment table with the look that only beagles can give: trusting brown eyes filled with concern. They seemed to say: What are we gonna do about this puppy that I've got sticking part way out? I've tried pushing, and it's not working.

The owner was a big man, well over six feet tall, and probably weighed 250 pounds. He was a trucker also, and wore a trucking company jacket and a Peterbuilt ball cap. He was very upset that his favorite rabbit dog was having trouble delivering this litter. He was sweating and nervous.

"She's never had trouble before, Doc. This is her third litter with the same male."

The lanky teenage boy that came with him was watching from a distance. He, like most people, was unsure whether he wanted to watch something that might involve seeing even a drop of blood.

It was ten o'clock at night, the office was dark except for the treatment room, and my only assistance would come from these guys.

"Can you hold her head for me while I check out the problem?" I asked.

"No sweat."

I put on a glove, squirted some lube on it, and inserted a finger, passing it around and lubricating the protruding pup. It was still alive but wouldn't last long if we didn't get it out, and pronto. I added more lube and worked it around the pup. Then I grabbed it and applied some gentle traction downward and, "pop." Out she came. The usual fluid followed, and I think I could hear the mother breathe a sigh of relief.

I looked up and said, "Good, that should be the end of the problem for now." I thought this would bring a happy response from the pair, but when I looked at the father, something was wrong.

The big man was going down. His face was whitish-green and his eyes were rolling up. I dropped the pup next to her mother, grabbed the dad's coat, and guided his rapid descent to the floor. I kept his head from whacking the linoleum, and when I looked up at the son, I saw that his face had turned bright red, and tears were streaming down it.

"HE'S DEAD!" the teenager screamed, his eyes as big as saucers. He began to cry uncontrollably.

"He's not dead; he just fainted. Help me get his feet elevated. Hand me that step stool."

"He's dead. I know it. Look at him."

"He'll be fine. Hand me that stool." The trucker put his hand to his head as the kid continued to sob. "Look, he's moving. He's OK," I said.

Then the dogs in the kennel began to howl along. They never howl. The boy was still crying as his dad woke up. He looked up at his son and said, "What's the matter with you?"

"I thought you were dead," the kid sobbed.

"I'm fine. I just got a little overwhelmed. Stop crying. I'm fine."

I looked up at the treatment table and noticed that, while these two humans had been putting on their performance, the unattended little beagle had delivered another pup, and was nursing them both.

Unexpected

"Rob, there's a man on the phone who says his dog has 'dropped a seed.' He says he snagged it on a fence. Is that an emergency?" Melissa asked.

"I'll bet it is! Have him come right in." My guess was that the seed he referred to was a testicle. If I were a dog and I'd just "snagged my seed" on a fence, I would appreciate quick action.

"He says he can be here in about an hour. He lives up on Pine Top Road on the other side of Bainbridge. Isn't that near Pike Lake?"

"Yup. We camped there a couple of years ago. There's a horse camp there too that you'd like. You can park your camper and tie your horse next to it. There are miles of horse trails back through the park. He must be from back in those hills."

We went back to routine office calls until the injured dog and his owner arrived. They were quite a pair. The man was thin, dressed in dirt-covered bib overalls that looked well broken in, and had a three-day beard on a face that was much taller than wide. The dog was a redbone coonhound with feet the size of coffee-can lids. He'd covered a lot of woods in his day, and had the body scars to prove it.

I looked under the dog and there, dangling like a banjo clock pendulum, was a green testicle. Green. I had never seen a bright green testicle.

"When did your dog get hurt?" I asked.

"Four days ago," was the response.

Assuming that the color was due to a disinfectant that had been applied, I wondered if it were Koppertox. This was a bright green topical treatment for hoof disease in horses. If it was Koppertox, the green mystery was solved. "What have you been doing since it happened?" I asked (meaning, what have you been doing in the way of treatment?).

Indignantly, he snapped back, "Baling hay."

Mystery solved. It was green because it was rotting. But the man's response caught me by surprise.

I've been taken by surprise in other instances. I recall one unforgettable case involving a dog that had been hit by a car.

A woman and her five-year-old daughter presented a young puppy that was unconscious and bleeding from its mouth and ears. She had literally been run over by a neighbor's car. I had the owner and her daughter wait in an exam room while I took the pup to the treatment area to try to do something for her. Before we could start the intravenous fluids and treatment for shock, she died.

I walked into the exam room and said, "I'm sorry, but your puppy just died. She was never conscious and died peacefully."

The little girl, with tears streaming down her face, said something I'll never forget. "Isn't it nice, Mommy? Fuzzy is the first member of our family in heaven."

What a wonderful ending. The child with the grown-up religious outlook had just given a lesson in faith.

The mother in the floor-length skirt with her hair pulled rigidly back from her face said, "Don't be ridiculous. There are no dogs in heaven!"

I was incredulous. I was so mad I couldn't respond. It was bad enough that this little girl had just lost her puppy, but now she'd been hurt again. By her own mother!

"Why would you say that?" I fumed.

"The Book of Revelations says that the dogs will be left outside the gates of the city. They will be there with the murderers, the sexually immoral, the idolaters, and those who practice magic arts."

What a fun lady. I wanted to ask her if all the nasty mothers would be outside the gate too, but I didn't. Religion was not to be argued. This was her child and her religion and it was not my place to comment. It was not my place to level the blast of sarcastic comments that came to mind. It was not my place to call child protective services and have them find out if this kid lived in a dungeon in the hills.

It made me wonder if all people who read the Bible in detail felt this way. For the next several months I asked every clergyman who came to the office if they felt there were dogs in heaven. It became an obsession with me. I asked Presbyterian, Methodist, Church of Christ, Baptist (3), and Pentecostal ministers. I asked two Catholic priests. I asked Evangelical United Brethren, Nazarene, and Bible Baptist preachers. I asked the part-time clergy of very small churches, and I listened to the Rev. Billy Graham. They were all of one opinion: If it wouldn't be heaven for you if your dog were not there, then your dog will indeed be waiting there for you.

Don't worry, kiddo. Fuzzy's waiting for you. I'm waiting

for your mother. I want her to tell me how the lions can lie down with the lambs if there are no animals in heaven.

On a twisty motorcycle road that I frequently ride early on Saturday mornings, at the very back of a yard in Sinking Spring, is a white wooden cross with "Kutie" painted on it. When I see it, I think of the little girl and Fuzzy. I also think of Robert Louis Stevenson, who said, "You think those dogs will not be in heaven! I tell you they will be there long before any of us."

Tale
End

You're about to read the final three stories, so this is my last chance to talk directly to you about the value of animals in our lives.

Last weekend, as my family and I were camping and s'mores were being prepared, I watched as an elderly woman in a wheelchair, cradling an old dog on her lap, was pushed by our campsite. I made a remark about the pair to my neighbor in the next camper and he replied, "That's my mother-in-law and that dog's just what she needs. Another damn thing to take care of when she can't even take care of herself!"

It was obvious to me that the dog *was* just what she needed. Animals stick by us "in sickness and in health, for better or worse, richer or poorer, as long as they live," and they don't even need the vows, the ring, or the cake. Our pets accept us, flawed as we are. They look at us and think we are simply terrific when few others do. We have no "past" in their eyes, only the present. And in that present we are perfect and hold great promise.

Animals never criticize us, and they offer limitless for-giveness—a kind of grace when we don't deserve it. They let us know that no matter what kind of person we may be, no matter how we fall short, they accept and love us. Wait a minute—haven't I heard all this somewhere before? Maybe . . . in church? Is it possible that, as the hymn says, "the Lord God made all creatures great and small" to give us some of the same kind of love offered by the Creator himself? No dogs in heaven? Maybe heaven is in the dog.

Animals can put things in perspective, keep us on an even keel, and make the darkness bright again. In the final assessment, those hours spent with animals can be very important ones in our lives.

So take good care of your friends. Domestic animals don't do as well by themselves as they do around people who care. Bad things can happen. Strays are hit by cars. Unvaccinated dogs and cats die needlessly from disease. Horses starve from neglected winter feeding programs. When left to their own devices, domestic animals really take a beating from Mother Nature. But together, man and animals can make a great team and really help one another.

Now why are these last three stories set off by them-selves? Because this is where they seem to belong. Even a kid can recognize the caboose!

Brave Heart

Nature hates a void. Earth tilled for a garden, left unat-tended, will fill with weeds. A forest clear-cut by loggers will in time regenerate. A surgeon who removes a tumor must obliterate the dead space left in its place or fluid will collect there and inhibit healing. Nature will fill a void.

Some of us are more natural than others. We hate to have dead space too. If a garage is empty, we fill it. If an attic is empty, it won't be empty for long. If we move from a small house to a big one, of course we fill it up. This makes it damn near impossible to downsize again, once the "collecting" begins. If you have enough room, you reach Collector Eldorado, a golden state in which nothing good needs to be gotten rid of ever again. Ever.

A corollary of this theorem of "void filling" can be applied to cats. Once you have a cat and realize how wonderful it is, another one is certainly no more trouble, and now you have twice the fun. They are pretty self-sufficient, not emotionally needy, and they don't cost much to maintain. If you live in an apartment, three or four may soon be living with you. If you live in a large house, six or seven are no problem. But if you live in the country, you need to be careful. Cats can expand to fill the available space.

Carol and Clayton Caldrone have twenty-two cats. Living on a picturesque farm in the rolling hills south of town, the cats have a perfect place to play. Woods for hunting, large green fields to explore, barns to prowl, and owners who love them. Cat Eldorado.

There is a problem with this perfection, though. Carol and Clayton have a lot of void to fill in the buildings on the farm. There's a chicken house, a large outbuilding, and a pole barn used as an office, filled with tables and desks and enough books to stock the Peebles library. In addition, there are several other smaller buildings, and of course, the house. These are great places for the cats to entertain themselves, and also to put all the stuff that is just too good to throw away. This, by itself, is no problem at all. Carol is an authority on clutter and its disposition. She has read, edited, and written on the subject. So there is no clutter in any building, just the largest and most organized mass of "stuff" in Adams County. Organized clutter. Is that an oxymoron? Cat Eldorado in Collector Eldorado.

The problem is this: When it's time for the cats to have their annual vaccinations, we not only have to round them up, we're forced into playing hide-and-seek in an environment that gives the cats every advantage. They hide in this mass of boxes, toys, wood, glass, metal, carpet, farm tools, books, and miscellaneous good stuff—and we seek. Twenty-two hiders, two seekers. Sounds unfair to me.

I don't usually make house calls for small animals. This is the exception. Bringing twenty-two cats to the office from sixteen miles away would be very difficult, requiring many trips. It's more reasonable for me to make one trip to the farm. It's also a beautiful drive down a couple of the most scenic roads in the county, so why wouldn't I go? It's a trip to treat a "herd" unlike any other.

Over the years we've tried different techniques to minimize trauma to the two teams. We've limited the playing field, first to only the chicken house (the most clutterless large mass of construction supplies is stored there) and an outbuilding filled with the boxes that once contained mail orders and Christmas gifts. Twenty or thirty years of Christmas gifts. The boxes come in handy for shipping, or for repacking to reduce clutter, and can't be disposed of. Then the field was narrowed to the chicken house and the office building. Then to the chicken house and the house itself. This year there will be a new attempt at making the game fair. All the cats will be somewhere in the house.

The rules are simple. The chubby, happy, well-adjusted and friendly cats, mostly tailless by the way, are going to put on their game faces and are allowed to bite, scratch, bolt, and elude capture by any means at their disposal. The seekers are allowed to fumble, crawl on their hands and knees, move tons of stuff, curse, and use needles to vaccinate the opponents. The game is won by the seekers if all cats are found and vaccinated. The hiders win if one of their team members can't be found, or if a seeker is sent to the emergency room. This has happened twice. Let the annual game begin.

"Dr. Sharp, don't forget that you're going to Carol's house to vaccinate the cats today," Melissa reminded me as I finished a cat castration. "She says that they're almost all in the house and it should be easy this year."

"Wishful thinking, I'm sure. I remember last year when we went into the chicken house. The boxes that were built along the wall for hens to lay eggs in had five cats curled up and sleeping in them. This is gonna be easy, I thought. Wrong. When we grabbed the first cat, the others launched out of there like horses out of the starting gate at the Kentucky Derby. They smelled the rat immediately and found places to hide in Carol's collections of stovepipes, fenceposts, and tin-roof metal trimmings."

"Didn't you get them all, though?"

"Of course, but Carol logged two miles on her knees under the tables and around the boxes of junk. All the while, both of us were swatting bumble bees the size of ping pong balls.

Carol's favorite cat, Blackie, is always the hardest to

vaccinate. He's a fourteen-pound, beautiful black Manx, and a bear to deal with. He's normally a real softy, sweet and gentle in every respect, but on game day a transformation occurs. He goes wild at the sight of strangers bearing needles, and becomes very wary, very fast, and not above retaliation. Once we get him, it's all downhill from there. (Blackie, of course, is the team captain of the Hiders. He leads by example and plays like Dick Butkus or Howie Long. Opponents fear him. Blackie the Brave.)

"I'll call Carol and tell her you're on your way."

I pulled into the driveway and parked next to the farmhouse. The view behind the house is spectacular. Rolling green hills, woods, a pond, a barn in the distance, and no other visible human contamination. If I were a cat, this is where I would want to live (not bad for humans either).

Gathering my bag of syringes and vaccine bottles, I went up on the back porch and prepared for the contest. Carol met me at the back door. "I have a couple over in the office. Why don't we start there?"

We walked across the driveway and into a very modern business office that, from the outside, looks like a pole barn. I mixed the vaccines on a desktop next to a computer while Carol picked up the cats. Three attempts, three successes, no sweat. "Did you get them all in this year?"

"Well, it took a while, but all the rest are in the house. I thought we could shut the doors and do them room by room. Do you have your usual list?"

"Yup. I'll cross them off as we go, so we don't miss anyone."

I set up operations on the kitchen table and mixed vaccines, opened syringes, and prepared the injections. When I was done, the search began. Within minutes, we were on our stomachs under the bed in a downstairs bedroom using flashlights around a mammoth storage box, in hot pursuit of a good hider. She was no match. We got her. Three in the family room gave up without a fight. Two more on the porch and one under the coat rack were crossed off.

"The rest are upstairs. I think it's going well, don't you?"

"Absolutely. Where's Blackie?"

"He's probably upstairs. He's seems to know when something's going on."

Room by room we searched and vaccinated, crossing the names off our list as we went. FBI agents with a search warrant couldn't have been more thorough. We searched in closets, around the shoes, in cupboards, in drawers, in the bathroom, behind and under furniture, and found cats, camouflaged and hiding. We were winning. As the list narrowed, it became obvious that Blackie hadn't yet been found.

One daring cat made a break for it down the upstairs hall. Moving at high speed, she arrived at the top of the stairs, and without slowing down, launched herself from the top step. She cleared the long, steep flight of stairs in one amazing leap and landed on the rug at the bottom. She kept running, and disappeared out of sight. Future trouble.

"We're making good time. Only Blackie and Minilynx the Leaper are left. Where do they usually hide?"

"Mini will probably be in the living room. That's where she goes when she's scared. Blackie will be back in the kitchen. I usually give him his medicine there, and maybe he'll be waiting for us."

Mini was behind the couch. She was a great jumper, but a lousy hider. We vaccinated her, and were down to one. Blackie was standing in the middle of the kitchen floor. He saw no need to hide.

"Here, Blackie. Come on Blackie," Carol coaxed.

Syringes in hand, I waited at a distance. The final score was at stake.

"Come on, Blackie, come here, Blackie, honey."

He looked at me and stared defiantly. His eyes burned as he hissed and stood his ground. He knew what we wanted and he saw no reason to surrender. Carol reached out and grabbed him, assuming that her familiarity with him would protect her from attack. When she placed him on the table, he let out a scream that was designed to intimidate. I grabbed the skin behind his neck to control him, stuck in the injections as quickly as possible, and listened as he made more terrifying cat sounds. His back feet were trying to claw his release, and as Carol reached down to try to calm him, he spun his head around and bit her hand (probably by mistake). Finished with my job, I let go of him and looked at the claw marks on my forearm as he leaped to the floor and took off.

"Are you OK?" I asked Carol.

"I need to scrub this in the sink. Wow, this really hurts!" she said, holding up a bleeding hand. Blackie had won the game on a technicality. Carol would need a trip to the emergency room, and antibiotics.

Blackie stood in the doorway and looked back as if to say, "I warned you more than once!"

Later that year, in an ironic twist of fate, Blackie the Brave, Blackie the Terrible, Blackie the Beautiful and Favorite, was also Blackie the Fragile. Cardiomyopathy had weakened his brave heart, and medication could no longer help him. In 2003, after a brief illness, Blackie was buried with full honors in a rock garden that overlooks his rolling farm.

Nature hates a void. No cat will ever replace Blackie,

but another will ascend to the level of favorite. Another little black tailless kitten will appear. The game will be played again.

Waiting

The old, blind cat sat on the exam table to have her blood glucose checked. Diabetes had taken its toll, and she was looking pretty weak.

"I'm telling you, Doc, when this one goes, there won't be another one. I just can't take this. I get too attached."

This is the second most common mantra that we hear (right after: he won't eat dog food, he thinks he's human).

Of course we get attached to our pets. If we didn't love them, we wouldn't have them. And when this old cat dies, a period of mourning will follow. A burial ritual, tears, and grief. Then a kitten will unexpectedly appear out of nowhere, and with Velcro paws, attach itself to us and create a new distraction. We don't want it. We won't keep it. But we can't let it starve.

Time will be kind, and while the new kitten provides entertainment, the pain of the loss of the old cat will fade to only good memories. We never can replace a pet we have lost, but we can add another friend. Different in many ways, yet in some ways the same. Our vow to never have another is forgotten.

What about animals? Do they become as attached to us? Do they experience feelings of loss when a human companion disappears from their lives? or is it simply the breaking of a habit and the disruption of old routines that they react to?

Bob McKinney lived with his daughter and an old yellow cat in a little house down by Serpent Mound. He had retired from farming when his Parkinson's disease left him without the strength or coordination to do his work. He gardened a little when he could, and liked to listen to baseball from his recliner in the living room. He knew the Cincinnati Reds and their stats like a play-by-play announcer. He never missed a game on television, and he had a radio next to the chair for the games that weren't televised. "Marty and Joe" were not just the announcers of the games, they were his window on the outside world.

Bob never listened to a game without his big yellow cat, William, in the chair with him. If Bob got too excited by the game and yelled at the umpire or players, William might move to the floor, but he was always nearby.

The Parkinson's progressed, and Bob eventually had to enter a nursing home. William stayed in Bob's chair, waiting for his friend to return. If William was in the house, William was in that chair.

The house was sold, Bob's daughter moved into an apartment in town with William, and he became a city cat. She took Bob's chair with her, and there William sat, waiting for his friend, and getting thinner by the week.

One day, Bob's daughter thought that he might like a visit from William, and after clearing it with the nursing home staff, she took William on a field trip. She carried the old yellow guy into Bob's room, and when he got near the bed, he jumped out of her arms and ran to Bob. He rubbed his head against Bob, and paced the bedsheets with his tail flagging. He was happy. He had found his friend.

Back home the next day, when William was let outside to "do his duty," he didn't return. Bob's daughter looked everywhere and called up and down the street. No William. That evening, a nurse from the facility called and said that a big yellow cat was on the front porch, and he looked a lot like the one she had seen visiting Bob McKinney. Was their cat missing?

Bob's daughter went over to see, and there was William, waiting at the front door of the nursing home. When she opened the door, William ran in, bolted straight down the hall, and jumped into Bob's bed.

Bob eventually died in the nursing home. William never stopped waiting in their favorite chair, waiting for his friend.

Devotion, and sadness caused by a loss can be found in other species, including some you might not have imagined. When Susie and I moved to Hillsboro, we bought an old Italianate Victorian brick house on Walnut Street. It was in need of repair, but was a wonderful old house. Twelve-foot ceilings, walnut woodwork, and a spot on the National Register of Historic Homes made this house worth the work to restore it. It needed a new roof, and this was the first of the major repairs. Next, the ornate soffit brackets that decorated the woodwork under the box gutters needed repair, and Jerry Adams was the carpenter selected for the job. He reproduced the originals that had been damaged, and repaired the wood under the box gutters. They were perfect, and could now be painted.

In the process of repairing the wood at the top of the house, a hole was found that pigeons had started to inhabit. Aside from the unsightliness of the white splats everywhere that accompany pigeons, the droppings are a known culture medium for the fungal disease, histoplasmosis, common in humans and pets in the Ohio River Valley. The pigeons had to go. I wasn't worried about the disease risk. We just didn't want birds in the new woodwork.

While up on a thirty-foot ladder, Jerry cleaned out the hole in the wood, evicted the pigeons, and repaired the area. The two pigeons circled the old homestead.

That evening, one of the pigeons landed on Walnut Street and was hit by a passing car. He was dead on impact and remained in the road. His mate circled, then she landed in the road and sat by the side of the dead bird. I saw a car pass right over the pair, and I couldn't believe it. If she didn't move, there were going to be two dead birds in the road.

I went out into the street, picked up the dead pigeon, and carried it to the grass. The other pigeon circled overhead, and after I was gone, she landed. She sat by the side of her mate, waiting.

I don't even like pigeons, but I'd only wanted them gone, not dead. Now this bird was making me feel guilty about something that I had every right to do. The next day, she was still by his side in the grass. This was going to stop. I went out and dug a hole in the garden and buried the dead bird.

The pigeon stayed in the yard for a few more days and then vanished, but during that time, I had a chance to think about devotion and attachment. Most birds will fly off if you toss a pebble in their direction, because it's a natural survival instinct. But even a one-ton car passing overhead could not make that pigeon leave her fallen mate.

Somewhere, that bird, like William, may still be sitting, waiting.

When we think of loyalty, the dog first comes to mind. The dog's dedication to his master is legendary. Heroic tales of dogs giving their lives to save humans could fill volumes. War dogs have been known to stay with fallen soldiers since the days of Hannibal and before. Not all of this is blind loyalty, but it shows intelligent intent.

Like William the cat, Tootsie Altiero was devoted to her master. She was an overweight, elderly Yorkie with a flea allergy that caused her to be brought to the office frequently for treatment. Her owner Tony was a gentleman in his late seventies who lived alone, except for Tootsie. They were a good match. Tony was in poor health and Tootsie helped him keep his mind on other things. He was still able to drive, and Tootsie was always willing to ride. Anywhere. They hadn't been apart in fifteen years.

One night, a tragedy occurred. Tony's house caught fire. By the time the trucks arrived, the little house was engulfed in flames. Firefighters worked their way into the living room, only to find Tony in his chair already overcome by the inferno. Tootsie was on his lap, defending him in death, snarling at her yellow-suited attackers. A firefighter grabbed her with his huge gloves and took her outside near the trucks for some fresh air. She jumped from his arms and, in an effort to run back into the house and to Tony, was hit by a car while crossing the road. Brought to the office by the fireman, she was too badly injured to survive. As she lay on the treatment table, coughing and taking a few last breaths, I thought about Tony and his valiant little defender who would rather burn to death than leave her master.

Now the outcome would be the same anyway. Maybe somehow she knew that they were going on one last trip together, and she didn't want to keep Tony waiting.

The Job

"What do you want to be when you grow up, kiddo?"

"I want to be a vet because I love animals," is the usual reply.

Frankly, who doesn't love animals? We own dogs and cats, ride horses, milk cows, feed ducks, and we go to the zoo in our spare time to look at the animals that we can't pet. I would never trust a person who dislikes animals. You're probably reading this because you love animals. Because kids seem to have a special fascination with them, becoming a veterinarian is one of the most common answers to the big question.

As we left elementary school and grew up, some of us still wanted to be veterinarians. We jumped through the hoops, and upon graduation, entered practice to help animals. Dogs had fractures, cats were sneezing, cows went down with milk fever, horses went through barbed-wire fences, pigs weren't eating, and we wanted to help them all.

But the puppy with the big soft eyes has something attached to it. It can't be removed. It's a human, and comes as an accessory that wasn't ordered. It's a third-party provider that makes every decision regarding the patient. Some owners are poor, some rich, some care a great deal, some are totally indifferent. All must be dealt with in some way.

After you've owned a practice for a number of years, and suffered the stress of paying employee salaries, drug bills, utilities, taxes, mortgages, and your accountant, you begin to realize that the animal's owner is indeed whom you work for, not the animal. If you make the animal well in the process, that's good too. You must be in business to make money or you won't be in business at all. For years you discuss the animal's problem in terms of satisfying the owner—and then something happens.

One day, a phone caller asks you what it would cost to go down to Grandpa's farm and euthanize three dogs, five cats, and a horse. It seems they live in the city and Grandpa died. Or a poor young couple brings in their dog which was hit by a car and has a rear leg hanging by a piece of skin. They say they can't afford to fix her and will you please put her to sleep? As you put the needle containing euthanasia solution in her vein, she gently licks your hand. You think to yourself, no damn way am I doing this. I'll amputate her leg and they can pay what they can afford. You remove the needle and talk some more. And you tell the city people to "take a little responsibility and don't expect me to be the easy way out."

The pendulum has swung back in favor of animals over humans again. You remember why you wanted to be a veterinarian in the first place. You begin to take the animal's side when decisions concerning treatment are discussed. You realize that when a puppy has a broken leg, the cost and aftercare can be worked out so that even a child could afford and accomplish it. By taking the animal's side you approach being an animal advocate.

Eventually you come to realize that the immutable bond between animals and man must be handled as a delicate balance. You realize that to swing weight in either direction can be questionable and that it is the balance itself which needs to be found in almost all cases.

This realization usually comes when your hair is gray, or gone, when you can't examine a dog on the floor without grabbing the exam table to get up, when you can't palpate a herd of Holsteins in a morning because the arthritis in your hand won't permit it.

In short, you become what you started to become so many years before: A veterinarian. You solve problems for both people and animals and you try to do it for the benefit of both. Neither animal advocate nor businessperson.

The stories you've read are only frames taken from a long movie that continues to run. They are not connected in any particular way, but they show that veterinarians are not just animal doctors. We must sometimes be psychologists, businesspeople, hand-holders, mind-readers, benefactors, detectives, and in some cases, crime-scene investigators. Every case is different. Every day is different. Every animal, with its attached owner, is a unique pair.

The expectations are simple. Make the animal well *and* make the owner happy. Every time. Walking that tightrope can be a challenge. I still feel lucky that I've been able to work in an environment that allows me, at all times, to be in the company of animals.

"What do you want to be when you grow up, kiddo?"

Index